baby
milestones

baby

Dr Carol Cooper

milestones

What to expect and how to stimulate
your child's development from 0–3 years

hamlyn

To my three wonderful sons, who never fail to amaze me.

First published in 2006 by Hamlyn,
a division of Octopus Publishing Group Ltd
2–4 Heron Quays, London E14 4JP

Distributed in the United States and Canada
by Sterling Publishing Co., Inc.
387 Park Avenue South, New York,
NY 10016-8810

ISBN-13: 978-0-600-61354-1

ISBN-10: 0-600-61354-2

A CIP catalogue record for this book is
available from the British Library

Printed and bound in China

10 9 8 7 6 5 4 3 2 1

This book is not intended as a substitute for
personal medical advice. The reader should
consult a physician in all matters relating
to health and particularly in respect of any
symptoms which require diagnosis or medical
attention. While the advice and information
are believed to be accurate and true at the
time of going to press, neither the author
nor the publisher can accept any legal
responsibility or liability for any errors or
omissions that may be made.

Contents

0–12 weeks

3–6 months

6–9 months

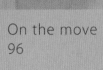

9–12 months

12–18 months

18–24 months

2–2½ years

2½–3 years

Foreword

Around 130 million babies are born every year. Given this statistic, having a baby is surely one of the most ordinary events in the world, yet it is still the most extraordinary thing that can happen to you. Once you have that new bundle of life in your arms, everything changes.

Why learn about baby development?

A parent's responsibility can seem awesome. Human babies are very immature and helpless at birth compared with other mammals. However, they develop quickly, and their individuality unfolds in a fascinating way. Because of this, there is a great deal that parents can do to stimulate the baby, guide their growth towards independence and bring out the best in their child.

Understanding how a baby develops and passes important milestones can help parents to handle the more challenging moments, of which there are always a few. Having this knowledge also makes parenting more much rewarding. These precious first 3 years with your baby never come back, so it is important, for the whole family's sake, to make the most of them. Finally, an appreciation of your baby's development enables you to stay ahead of the game and anticipate potential dangers, thus preventing accidents and keeping your baby safe.

Babies and parents are all individuals

Each baby is an individual and may not develop exactly according to a timetable. However, every baby develops in the same sequence, and it is still possible to give guidelines as to what to expect and when.

Babies have some characteristics that are decided before birth. Certain personality traits, for instance, may be inborn. That is why no two babies are ever entirely alike.

Some are contented; others are more demanding. Some are wakeful; others spend more time dozing. It is important to recognize your own baby's temperament and quirks, because you cannot turn your baby into someone else. As a parent, your brief is to accept your baby as she is, so that you can provide her with just the right amount of stimulation and encouragement to fulfil her own unique potential.

I am aware that parents are also individuals. Different people have different lives and, inevitably, that means different parenting styles. What works for one family may not work for another. Within these pages is the information that every parent needs about their baby's growth and development, so that they can make the choices that suit them best.

How to use this book

The Introduction covers a range of general topics, such as how babies learn, what kind of stimulation works best, and whether gender characteristics are inborn. It also includes information on issues that can arise if you have twins or triplets, or a premature or special-needs baby.

The bulk of the book is then arranged chronologically, in sections covering 0–12 weeks, 3–6 months, 6–9 months, 9–12 months, 12–18 months, 18–24 months, 2–2½ years and 2½–3 years. Within each of these there is an overview of what you can expect, a summary of development in chart form, and then five more detailed sections dealing with Growth and health, Motor development,

Senses and learning, Communication and, finally, Emotions. If your baby does not conform in every way to the descriptions given, there is no need to worry unduly, because babies differ. You will find guidance on what parents can look out for and what they can do about potential problems. Throughout the text, there is practical advice on stimulating your baby and choosing toys, as well as hints on health and safety. Panels cover topics such as teething, watching television and other issues that concern parents.

Much of this book is based on the advice I give as a family doctor to parents in my own consulting room every working day, and inevitably some is also based on my own experience as a mother of three children.

With a book, you can reach many more people than you ever can as a family doctor, no matter how hard you work. I wrote this book in the hope that you will enjoy being a parent, and that raising your baby proves to be a rich and rewarding experience for you and all your family.

Introduction

Your baby is not a blank page. He is born with a complete set of genetic material, half from each parent and all of it his very own. At birth he has five senses, basic reflexes, and the ability to move his limbs and to communicate on a basic level by crying. But he still has so much further to go.

Why parents are so important

Of all the species, the newborn human is the most helpless and immature. At first, your baby is incapable of independent living. He is utterly dependent on you for warmth, food, shelter and love.

It is hard to overestimate the importance of the early years. During these first 3 years, a baby grows from an average length of 51 cm (20 in) to a height of 93 cm (37 in) and, from his birthweight of about 3.5 kg (7 lb 11 oz), he gains around 11.5 kg (25 lb 5 oz). As your baby grows, his whole being becomes more and more complex. His physical growth is inextricably linked with his intellectual, social and emotional development.

As a parent, you are your baby's first line of protection against the world. You are also his first plaything, his first teacher, his first love. Babies learn by imitation. Even at a few days old, a baby sticks out his tongue if he sees you do it first. You are on every level his inspiration, his model. It is no exaggeration to say that his relationship with you moulds the pattern for every relationship he will ever have.

Babies learn through play, manipulating their surroundings in ever more skilled ways (see page 13). Parents can encourage exploration within safe surroundings, helping their baby to notice things, to find out how things work and to gradually make sense of the world. With your guidance, your baby also learns to understand others and to express himself.

Whatever your baby does, your positive feedback is essential. All babies develop best in a secure environment filled with love. There will be testing times over the years, but the loving parent tries to be patient and avoids offering undue criticism. Praise him when you can, so that he feels at ease with himself. Your baby will get things wrong. Let him know when this happens, but also let him know that it is fine to learn from his mistakes.

Providing the right amount of stimulation

Too little stimulation means that your baby may not develop to the full. There is evidence from both animals and humans that a poor environment can lead to poor learning. The stimulation a baby gets must match his needs. There are sensitive periods when he is most ready to acquire certain skills, for example learning to chew at around 6 months and learning bladder control from around 2 years. A baby who does not get any solid food by 6–8 months of age will have trouble learning to chew.

On the other hand, too much stimulation is bewildering. The 'hot-housed' baby will not learn new skills any faster, because his brain simply is not ready to take in so much information. A young baby who is shown flashcards and constantly stimulated will become fractious and tired. In the long run he may even be put off learning, making the whole exercise counterproductive.

Rates of development

Some babies develop more quickly than others. It is not clear why rates of progress differ, but they do. Trends can run in families: a toddler who is late in becoming dry at night may have a parent who was also later than average. Even so, all babies acquire skills in the same sequence: for instance, your baby will sit before he can stand.

Parents often think that passing milestones is a measure of intelligence, but this is not the case. Intellect has little bearing on, say, walking. In reality, a child's personality is more important than his IQ. If your baby is placid and laid-back, he may not practise new skills with the same enthusiasm as a baby who is determined to be independent. So the exact timing is less important than many parents think. However, talk to your health visitor or doctor if you have any concerns.

Pre-birth development

Over a period of 8½ months, a single cell, barely visible without a microscope, turns into the complex being that is your baby, ready to be born and face the world. At birth, your baby is made up of several thousand billion cells, reflecting the genetic blueprint contained in her DNA (deoxyribonucleic acid).

How your baby's organs develop

The brain and nervous system start off as a row of cells along your baby's back when she is still an embryo less than 3 weeks old. These cells turn first into a lengthwise fold, then into a cylinder called the neural tube. The neural tube divides into different parts: the top end becomes the brain, while the rest forms the spinal cord.

Brain and nerves

The nerve cells grow rapidly, and fibres called dendrites extend from each one. The largest trunk of fibre from each nerve cell is called an axon, and this sends

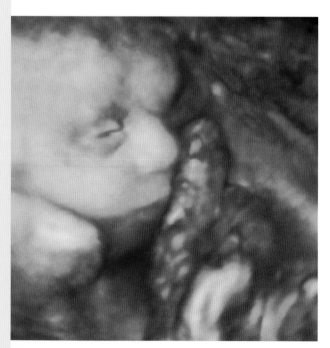

electrical signals from one nerve cell to another and from the nerve to the muscle. In the womb, the brain produces many more nerve cells than it needs. At birth, your baby has around 200 billion nerve cells. This is about twice as many as an adult. Development involves selectively letting many nerve cells die off and subsequently making new connections between those that remain.

Muscles and movement

Limbs first appear as tiny buds on each side of the embryo. These buds lengthen and develop nodules that become your baby's hands and feet.

Your baby's arms and legs start moving at about 10 weeks, and make increasingly gymnastic movements. As the nervous system develops and makes vital connections with the muscles, your unborn baby kicks her legs, opens and closes her fingers, sucks her thumb and even grasps her umbilical

DNA

In code form, DNA holds all the data needed for a baby to develop into an adult. Your baby gets half her DNA from each parent. Because there is a huge number of genes – about 100,000 in all – the number of possible combinations is almost unimaginably large, so the end-product is uniquely her own.

Nature versus nurture

Are all human traits inborn, or are they shaped by the environment in the early years of life? If you favour the inborn, or 'nature', theory, it follows that nothing you can do as a parent makes much difference. Your baby will be what she is destined to be, and she will learn whether or not you stimulate her. On the other hand, if you subscribe to the 'nurture' side of the argument argument, then your role as a parent is fundamental in shaping your baby's development.

There is no exact answer to this question, but it is likely that both nature and nurture are important in their own way. Take language acquisition. Babies learn to speak partly because of an innate ability and partly through mimicking those around them. This is why babies babble to themselves from an early age, but they also need to be spoken to in order to develop meaningful speech.

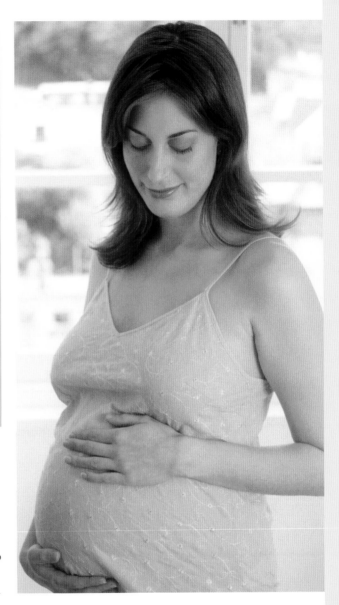

cord. As her face muscles start to mature, she tries out frowns, lip movements and other facial expressions.

The senses before birth

The ear is formed by 16 weeks of pregnancy, which is when your baby starts to hear. The sound of your voice, your heart, your lungs and the gurgling of your stomach are never far away. Research proves that the baby not only responds to sounds in the womb, but also remembers them afterwards. Immediately after birth, new babies know their mother's voice. They also recognize melodies they have heard in the womb, such as the signature tunes of some television programmes.

Your baby's eyes become light-sensitive at about 14 weeks of pregnancy. The eyelids stay shut until 22 weeks, but they are translucent, so your baby can distinguish between light and dark.

Your unborn baby constantly swallows amniotic fluid, along with traces of the foods that you eat. With these gulps, the 10,000 or so taste buds that your baby is born with enjoy their first tastes of your diet. Getting a baby used to the special taste of her mother's milk may help her with breast-feeding later.

How your baby develops and learns

As your baby develops, his brain cells link together to form circuits. His experiences literally mould his brain. Learning involves making new connections between the cells. Repeating an activity – seeing a picture in a book, or going upstairs on all fours – reinforces these connections. Everything a baby sees, hears, feels, smells or tastes leaves a subtle trace on his brain.

Growth and learning

Physical growth and development go hand in hand. A young baby learns at close range as he sees, hears, feels and smells you. His horizons are limited because he cannot see far or reach out with any accuracy, let alone get up and crawl. Your new baby does not find out much about the texture (or taste) of things until he is mature enough to reach out and grab them, and to put them in his mouth.

A baby's body develops from the head down. His neck and arms grow in size and strength before his hips and legs. This is why a young baby, who cannot sit up, uses his hands to explore whatever is within reach.

Once your baby sits up, his gaze lands on more distant things. He notices who is coming through the door and what people are eating. Now he is ready for social skills.

At the sitting stage, a baby's legs act as little more than stabilizers. He cannot walk until his trunk and hip muscles will support his weight. When he does walk, he can learn advanced lessons from objects that are further away.

Interlinking of skills

As time passes, your baby's skills become increasingly interlinked. His accurate grasp with thumb and forefinger depends on good vision as well as on coordination of his hand.

When he learns to wave goodbye, his general understanding has progressed, along with his senses and coordination. Waving is a simple muscular action, but it demonstrates social and emotional skills.

Learning through play

Play is vital to learning. It stimulates your baby's senses, especially vision, touch and hearing. It also helps him to acquire and practise coordination and other skills. A baby who is deprived of the opportunity to play may have learning difficulties later.

Toys

All toys are a source of experiment, but some encourage a baby to use his imagination more than others. Some toys provide an outlet for your baby's energies, or even help to release aggression. A baby needs a variety of toys, but they do not have to be expensive. Toys can be second-hand, if they are in good condition. You can wash most toys in sterilizing solution. Toys need not be elaborate. Very complex toys inhibit the imagination. The more active the toy, the more passive the child will be.

Your baby will enjoy playthings of different shapes, sizes and textures. He will make his own fun by building towers out of blocks and putting things into boxes. You do not have to play with him all the time, but give him attention or help when he needs it.

It is vital for your baby gradually to learn about sustained play. This improves his concentration, although it is just as important not to force him to keep playing with something once he loses interest in it.

Different types of play

Playing with other people helps a baby to socialize, cooperate, take turns, share and learn that rules exist. A child under 3 years old may not be ready to make real friends, but he can play alongside another child.

Almost any kind of role play helps his development. Old clothes from a dressing-up box or suitcase allow your child to try out being different people.

Creative play exercises the imagination. When your baby scribbles a picture for you, or offers you a lump of dough that he has modelled, it may not look like very much, but it is important to encourage him with positive feedback.

Boisterous play helps release pent-up energy and channel aggression. An outing every day helps your child experience new things as well as let off some steam.

Gender and family position

Everyone knows that boys and girls are different. Research shows that 10-month-old babies spend more time looking at pictures of babies of the same sex as themselves. When they meet another baby, they can tell his or her gender from body movements alone, not from clothes or hairstyle.

Gender differences

By 1 year, boys prefer noisy games and adventurous play. By 3 years, boys cry less and show less intimacy, explore more, often have better spatial awareness and are better at ball games. Girls tend to talk earlier and also often walk and become toilet-trained sooner. Girls are often quieter, agile and graceful, as well as more cooperative and patient.

There are obvious anatomical differences in their genitals, as well as in height, weight and strength. But how deep are the distinctions in behaviour and personality?

Parents respond differently to boys and girls. Mothers talk more to baby girls and hug them more. Later on, a boy may get recognition for being brave, while a girl is more often praised for being pretty or helpful. However, trying to redress the balance between the sexes works only to a point. The bottom line is that fundamental gender differences do exist.

Research shows that there are structural differences between the male and female brain. These may be due to the male hormone testosterone, which affects the growing brain as well as other organs. This is not necessarily the reason for all the differences. As parents, we respond to our baby's gender characteristics, but we also create many of them.

Avoiding sexual stereotyping

Innate gender differences, plus other influences, such as television and people outside the family, mean that you cannot entirely prevent stereotypical behaviour. However, you can gently guide your baby's early experiences.

If you have a son
- Cuddle him and encourage him to express emotions (such as pain when he is hurt).

- Have one-to-one conversations with him.

- Help him concentrate with books and other quiet pursuits. Play games that involve taking turns.

If you have a daughter
- Nurture her strengths.

- Encourage her to play physical games and to choose loose clothing that allows her to move freely.

- Give her opportunities to play with shapes, puzzles and construction toys.

- When reading to her, choose books that show girls and women succeeding.

Bringing out the best in your children

Only child
- Encourage her to meet other children.

- Avoid treating her like an adult.

First child
- Don't expect too much of your child.

- Allow her to be a child.

Second child
- Give her attention.

- Avoid babying her for too long.

Middle child
- Listen to her opinion.

- Let your child know she is special too.

Youngest child
- Let her have new things sometimes.

- Spend time with her.

Family position

A child's position in the family can have subtle effects. There are no absolute rules, but there are general trends.

First or only child

First-born children are achievers who are not easily deterred from what they want. Often highly strung, your first-born may be eager to please, reflecting many of your own anxieties and ambitions. Because you have the time to talk more to a first child, she may be likely to speak earlier than subsequent children.

The only child basks in exclusive attention. She speaks well and relates to adults. Life can be lonely and often she may lack confidence with other children. On the plus side, however, she grows up to be contented with her own company and is often a high achiever.

Second child

The second child enjoys a more relaxed upbringing. She has to fit in with family life, and she copes. Second-born children develop a sense of humour, but they may be very critical, especially of an older sibling, who appears to enjoy all the advantages.

Middle child

The middle-born child learns to juggle and negotiate. She gets on with everyone but can feel left out. There is nothing very special about her birth rank, and she may feel that she gets no special recognition from her parents.

Youngest child

The last-born child gets the least attention from her parents, and siblings tend to be role models. She accommodates everyone. Although she may achieve less academically, she is sensible, jolly and good-natured.

Twins and multiples

There is something very special about multiple-birth babies. If you have twins, triplets, or more, you are bound to be very proud. You will also be very busy. However, babies who are born more than one at a time face some drawbacks, and it is worth making an effort to help their development.

Advantages and disadvantages

Twins have each other for company, and it is lovely to watch them play together. However, the constant presence of a playmate can stop each twin socializing with other children, and it can affect learning as well. Sometimes, twins experience a delay in their language development, or they just have immature speech for longer. One reason may be that mistakes and mispronunciations simply get reinforced with practice between the babies, because they spend more time chattering to each other than speaking with an adult.

You can encourage language skills by spending one-to-one time with each of your babies. This gives each of them a chance to have uninterrupted conversations. Whether they are together or apart, make eye contact with the twin to whom you are speaking. It also helps to use each baby's name when addressing him, ideally at the start of each sentence as it will then be a cue for him to pay attention.

Help your twins learn to concentrate. It is hard for each baby to play with any one toy for long, because his twin gets in on the act, so twins can have trouble sustaining their attention. Again, this is where some time with each twin really helps. Separate outings now and again are ideal if you can manage this.

Twins as individuals

Growing up as an individual human being is a challenge for any twin or higher multiple. As twins grow up and learn to function as individuals, they also have the task of growing away from each other and establishing their own identity. This process is sometimes called 'individuation'. Treating twins as one indistinguishable unit often interferes with this.

You may want to banish the word 'twins' from conversations with and around your children. Everyone should learn to respect them and address them as individuals. This is especially hard with identical twins or triplets, as it can be nearly impossible to tell them apart. Dressing them in different clothing helps to maintain their own individuality, as does giving them different hairstyles if possible.

Treating your children as individuals

Treating your babies as individuals has many benefits, in both the short term and long term. It can:

■ Help their language and social skills develop.

■ Improve their behaviour and make discipline easier.

■ Reduce competition and fighting.

■ Make parenting more satisfying.

■ Make their school careers more productive.

■ Make adolescence less difficult.

■ Help them to grow into functional adults.

Identical twins are not the same

If you have identical babies, you may be thinking 'But they are the same'. However, the fact is that no two humans, even identical twins, are truly identical. They may have the same genes, but not all genes are expressed, and some lie dormant. And twins never have exactly the same pre-birth environment. Even when they share the same placenta and umbilical cord, the babies don't get exactly the same amount of blood and oxygen. During birth, each twin may have a different experience, which may mould his subsequent behaviour. These early influences can be very important, which may be why even so-called 'identical' twins can exhibit different personalities from the moment they are born. It is therefore best not to make assumptions about your babies' characteristics.

Coping with two or more babies

It can be very hard to find the time for each of your babies. The demands on a parent are much greater than with several closely spaced children, because twins and multiples often have the same needs – and at the same time. Enlisting help is essential. A reliable teenager could take one baby to the park sometimes, or you could share childcare with another family.

Parents with only one baby may not appreciate the pressures of parenting twins. Another parent of twins will understand, however. You could even swap a baby every so often, so that each of your twins gets some time without his sibling's constant presence.

Culture and environment

All babies thrive in an environment where they are shown love, in the form of smiles, kisses, chats, hugs and other forms of physical contact. A loving hug can even regulate a baby's heartbeat and breathing, and is the best possible stimulus for development.

Love and calm

Parents often show their love instinctively, but a few don't. Emotional deprivation can have lasting effects on a baby's social, emotional and intellectual development. Speech is most often affected, while motor milestones are generally least affected. When it is severe, emotional deprivation even stunts physical growth.

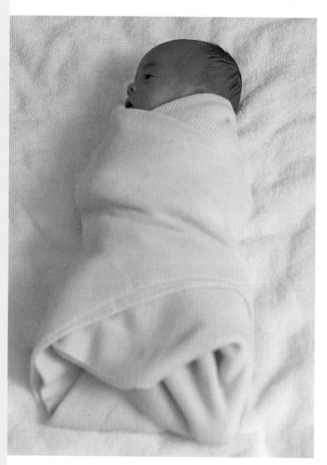

Babies also benefit from an element of calm. This does not mean that life must be boringly quiet. The occasional raised voice is inevitable and harmless. However, constant conflict undermines a child's sense of security and ultimately has similar effects to emotional deprivation.

A baby does best when she gets the stimulation that is right for her stage of development (see also pages 66–67). A dull environment starves the senses. The baby who spends long hours in one position in a cot or buggy has fewer opportunities to try out new skills. This happens to babies who are raised in institutions like orphanages. On a lesser scale, it can also happen at home, especially if the family is large, or the parents (or the single parent) are stressed or ill.

In some households, a mother may not see the need to let her baby tackle everyday tasks like dressing herself or using a spoon. The result is a young child who is totally dependent on others and who may lose the will to learn new things.

Cultural differences

Cultural differences influence development. In many societies, the father plays little part in child-rearing, remaining a distant and perhaps strict figure – or even being absent altogether. A baby may spend most of her time with her mother, grandmother, and aunts, only later becoming acquainted with male role models.

In some parts of the world, young children are not shielded from danger as they are in western countries. A baby may be allowed to handle knives and other implements. Such babies learn quickly to respect sharp tools, although there can be accidents along the way.

Some young babies are swaddled. This tight wrapping is thought to have a calming effect, and research shows it helps deep sleep. However, swaddled babies can overheat, especially in a home with central heating.

In many cultures, a baby is carried around for most of the first 12 months, usually by her mother. Being carried on the front, as is done in many parts of the world, not only leaves a mother's hands free but also keeps her baby in close contact both with her heartbeat and with the warmth of her body. This can have a calming effect, but sometimes babies get restless when carried like this.

In some south-east Asian countries, mothers make slings to carry their baby on their backs. In this way, the baby sees more of the world, which can be stimulating. However, she cannot move around much, so there are advantages and disadvantages.

In western countries, parents are more likely to carry a baby using a commercially made baby sling.

Using other carers

Many parents are concerned about having someone else look after their baby while they work. Even quality child care is not the same as spending time at home with one or both parents. However, there are positive aspects for you and your baby.

Variety of experience can enrich your child's social and emotional development. While with other carers, your baby may also come into contact with other children, which is especially valuable for an only child. Being at work can make you more fulfilled, so that you return home with renewed enthusiasm for parenting.

Take time deciding on childcare and choose the best that you can. This is not necessarily the most expensive option: it is the person whose experience most closely matches your ideas for your child, and the one with whom you feel most comfortable.

Rest assured that the concept of quality time really does seem to hold true. Going out to work does not damage the parent/child bond as long as the parent spends time comforting and playing with his or her baby every day.

Premature babies

Many babies are born too soon. It is natural for a parent to worry, but the outlook for premature babies, even very tiny ones, is improving all the time, so there is every cause for optimism.

The meaning of 'prematurity'

A normal pregnancy is about 40 weeks long. A premature baby is any baby born before 37 weeks in the womb. In the UK, for example, some 7 per cent of babies are premature. As in many other western countries, this figure has not changed for decades, despite ongoing advances in modern medical care.

If your baby is born prematurely, you may have concerns about feeding and bonding. When a baby is very small, even holding him can seem scary. And if he is in a special care unit, as many premature babies are, the high-tech equipment can be very daunting.

Not surprisingly, most parents in this situation cannot help being at least a little anxious about their baby's future, especially if he is very premature.

The causes of prematurity

Many things can trigger premature birth. Sometimes there is not enough blood flowing from the placenta to the baby. In some cases, an infection in the womb can trigger labour. Twins, triplets, and more, are especially prone to arriving early. In at least a third of cases, though, there is no obvious cause.

This means that there are no known ways to prevent many premature births. On the plus side, it also means that mothers should not blame themselves in any way, because there is nothing they could have done to stop it.

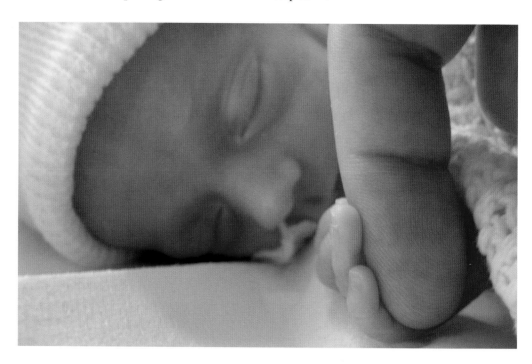

Developing ties that bind

It can be hard to develop an attachment to such a vulnerable scrap of human life. In fact, many parents worry about doing so, in case their baby does not survive. Fortunately, these fears are often misplaced, but they are a sign that you care.

Even if your baby is in a special care unit, it is good for you both to get to know each other. By taking part in everyday care, such as feeding and nappy-changing, you can comfort your baby. The staff on the unit can show you how best to hold and handle him. You may be able to lift him out of the incubator to snuggle against your chest. This kind of skin-to-skin contact allows your baby to feel and smell you. It can even calm your baby's breathing and boost his growth.

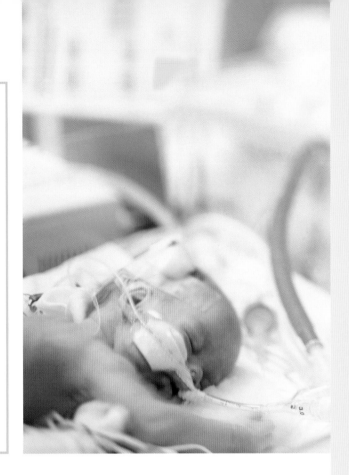

Caring for premature babies

Premature babies miss out on the final maturation time in the womb. Their bodies therefore have less fat, and many of their systems are immature. Babies born too soon have an extra need for warmth, nourishment and protection from infection. Many need help with breathing, because they may not have enough of an essential chemical, called surfactant, which helps air to pass into their lungs.

Some premature babies are so young that their sucking reflex has yet to develop. Feeds may need to be given through a tube that goes up the nose and then into the stomach. Even so, breast milk is usually still the best food because it contains nutrients, hormones and growth factors. It also has white blood cells that boost a vulnerable baby's defences against infection. If anything, premature babies need these even more than a baby born at full term. This is why you will be encouraged to breast-feed if at all possible, even though you may need to express milk so that it can be fed to your baby by tube.

What prematurity means for your baby's future

Leaving the womb ahead of schedule does mean that a baby starts off at a different point and so will be lighter and smaller than average. However, premature babies can catch up very quickly. Some stay petite, but most grow to a normal size. In fact, by the age of 2 years, there is often little difference between a baby born at term and one who arrives too soon.

In terms of development, you can expect a baby born, say, 8 weeks early to be more like a 4-month-old when he reaches 6 months. You need to take this into account and avoid comparing him with other babies. The discrepancy becomes less marked over time and, all being well, ultimately evens out.

21

Special-needs babies

The term 'special needs' is used for any child whose development, communication, learning skills or behaviour are such that she needs special provision to realize her potential. It covers a wider range of conditions and is much more positive than the older 'handicapped' and 'disabled'.

Adjusting to the news

It can be a huge blow to discover that you have a special-needs baby. Both you and your child may need long-term help and guidance. Whether you are looking for medical, practical or emotional support, talk to your health visitor, family doctor or paediatrician. The paediatrician is the medical specialist who usually diagnoses a problem and decides that a child has special needs, but teamwork is very important and generally involves many different professionals, each offering their own expertise. If your child has cerebral palsy, for instance, a physiotherapist is part of the team. For other conditions, the team might include a child psychiatrist. Even though there may be other adults involved, none of this detracts from the fact that, as the parent, you are still the most important person in your baby's life.

Development and learning

A special-needs baby may develop more slowly than average, and she may struggle to master very basic skills. Nonetheless, there will be successes. It is important to focus on what your baby can do, not what she cannot do. It may be that you have to make the most of your baby's other senses. For instance, children who are partially sighted rely more on touch, hearing and smell.

However you do it, celebrate every milestone. Positive feedback shows that you care and makes a dramatic difference to how a baby feels about herself. Time, attention and loving encouragement can increase any child's achievements, even if she has a profound handicap. This, in turn, makes parenting more rewarding, and will strengthen the bond between you and your child. It is an upward spiral that feeds a child's success and boosts your confidence as a parent.

Although few parents would choose to have a special-needs baby, many discover in time how extraordinarily satisfying it can sometimes be. The future for a special-needs child need not be bleak. With the right environment and stimulation, many grow up to lead fulfilling lives.

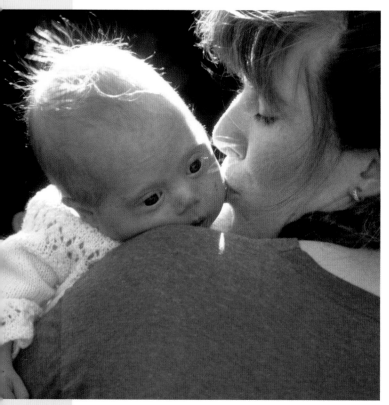

Coping with special needs

In some ways, having a special-needs baby is a bereavement because you have lost the chance of a normal parenting experience. Like other kinds of grief, you may go through several stages. These include:

☐ Initial shock on hearing the diagnosis.

☐ Denial or inability to believe it.

☐ Anger at yourself, your partner, or health professionals that you feel have failed you.

☐ Intense sadness or depression.

☐ Finally, acceptance that you can lead a family life with a special needs child.

The process varies from person to person, even within a couple, and it can take many years.

Finding support

A well as good days, there will be not-so-good days, when you feel tired and less positive. Feeling drained or low is entirely understandable, and this is where support groups come into their own.

Meeting another family in a similar situation to your own can be an excellent source of emotional comfort and practical know-how. For some parents, it is nothing short of inspirational.

Many support groups have local branches or a helpline. Some charities even offer support for very rare conditions that no other baby seems to have. There are web-based resources too, but you need to be discerning about the information on the internet.

In terms of parenting, the burden of caring for a special-needs baby is usually heavier than average, emotionally, physically and possibly financially. It is important that you get whatever support you need for yourself, not least so that you can do your best for your family.

0–12 weeks

Your new baby

Major milestones

- ✔ Develops head control
- ✔ Produces first smile
- ✔ Loses early reflexes
- ✔ Lies flat rather than in the fetal position
- ✔ Follows moving objects with eyes
- ✔ Turns head towards sounds

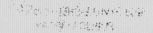

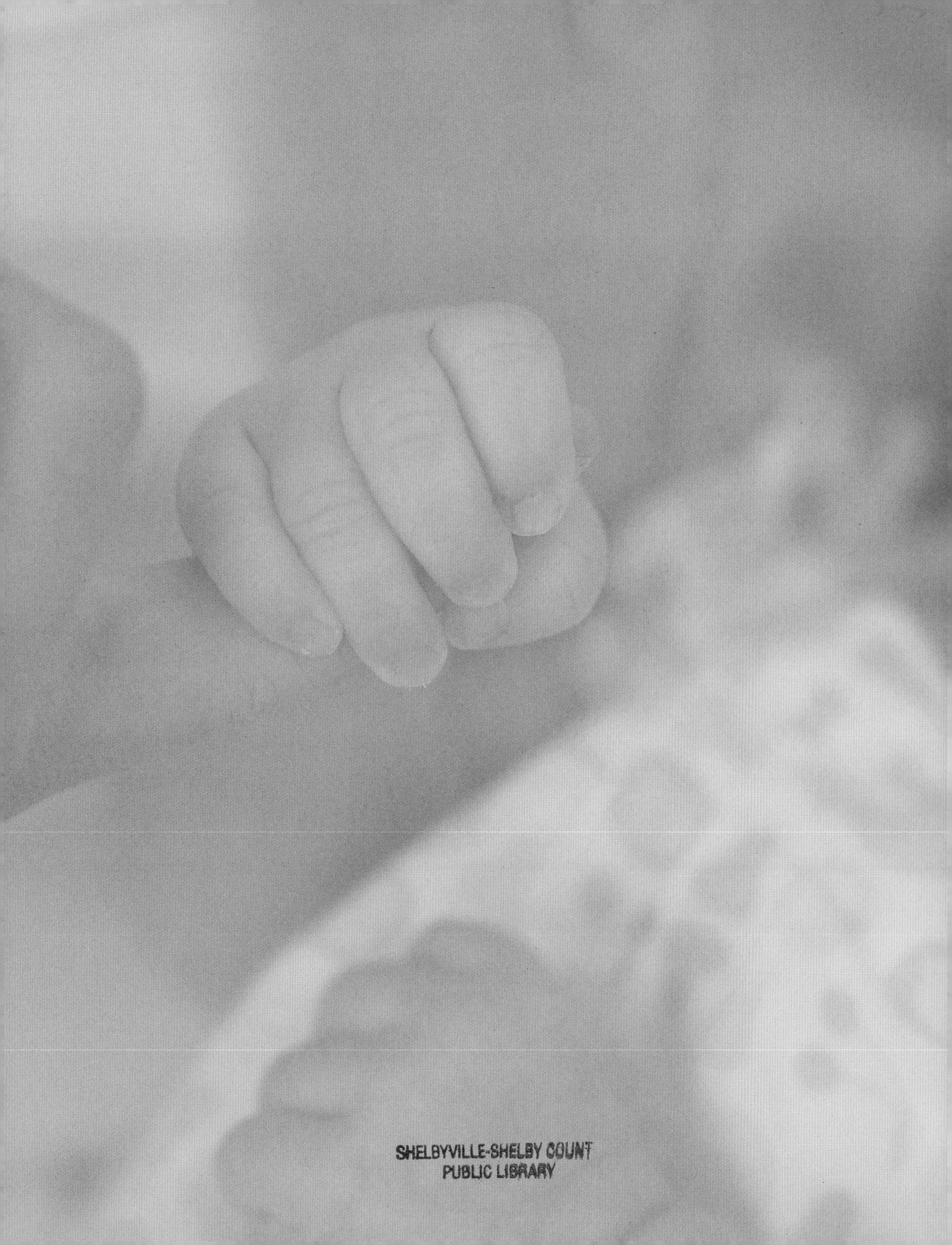

Things to look out for

Your baby's first 3 months are an amazing time of discovery. At birth, his vision is immature, he cannot manoeuvre his own body, and he cannot tell you what he wants, except by crying.

Physical changes

Your baby's appearance changes a lot in the first 3 months. He grows in size, and there are other developments too. By 12 weeks, his skin is less red and the blue eyes he had at birth could be turning brown. His body slowly uncurls from the fetal position, and his head becomes less lop-sided.

The early reflexes of the newborn gradually fade away, to be replaced by more purposeful movements as his nervous system matures and his muscles gain strength. He often kicks his limbs. He also tries to reach out for things, although not always successfully. Trial and error are a normal part of the process.

Soon, your baby learns to control his head and his neck. By 12 weeks, he can hold his head erect in readiness to discover new horizons.

Your baby and his environment

It may not always be obvious, but your baby is busy developing new skills with awesome speed. Every moment you spend with him matters. Each day brings something new.

To begin with, he focuses on what is nearest to him – you. His innate attachment to you deepens as he gazes at you for ages, drinking in your smell and your taste. He feels your warmth and learns all the subtleties of your voice. This is a perfect game plan for his survival and development.

Within the limits of his vision, your baby studies whatever he can – the edge of his cot, the mobile above his head, the light from the window. He observes human faces especially closely and soon responds with a variety of expressions. When he gives his first genuine smile, at around 6 weeks, you show your delight, prompting more smiles from him.

Communicating

Your baby can localize sound well and listens to you intently. Although he does not always respond, he takes everything in. What he hears profoundly shapes the sounds he learns to make. As the weeks pass, his repertoire of noises expands. He no longer simply cries, although when he does, his cries are more varied. He also sighs, gurgles and coos, experimenting with a range of vowel sounds.

If you express your joy at these sounds, he will respond by making more sounds. Before long, you will find that you are having mini-conversations together. These strengthen the bond between you both and stimulate his development.

In the first few weeks, he may cry a great deal. Nights are disturbed for feeds and also for the simple reason that your new baby does not yet have a routine. Babies are not all alike, and some cry more than others. However, babies cry less from the second month onwards. You, in turn, relax more, even if your baby does not yet allow you a full night's sleep. At 6 weeks, your baby already seems more settled. You have got to know each other.

Your baby displays his emotions readily. At first, he just cries to show how he feels. However, as the weeks pass, he makes eye contact more and learns to use his face to express surprise, pleasure, discomfort and other feelings.

Being a parent

This time is a voyage of discovery for you as well as your baby. If you are a new parent, it can take time to adjust to your new role, even though you are thrilled about the arrival of your baby. You may also have concerns about your baby's appearance or behaviour: is this what to expect from him at this time?

The rest of the family, your partner included, also need attention. If this is your second or subsequent baby, you may have to fit caring for the new arrival into an already packed schedule.

Summary of development

Growth and health

At birth
- Head is about a quarter of the body length.
- Head may be flattened on one side or even bullet-shaped from the birth.
- Hair may be coarse.

- Skin is soft, reddish, and often covered in vernix (see page 30).

0–8 weeks
- Anterior fontanelle (soft spot at front of head) enlarges.

0–12 weeks
- Hair and nails grow rapidly.

By 12 weeks
- Posterior fontanelle (soft spot at back of head) can hardly be felt.

- Body skin is paler and smoother, although scalp may be scaly with cradle cap.

Care

0–2 weeks
- Sleeps much of the time.

0–6 weeks
- Needs frequent small feeds.

By 6 weeks
- More obvious periods of sleep and wakefulness develop.

Motor development

At birth
- Has little or no head control.
- Holds fists shut tight, and arms and legs bent.
- Has many primitive reflexes – sucking, rooting, grasping, startle, stepping.

0–6 weeks
- Primitive reflexes gradually disappear.

0–12 weeks
- Neck muscles strengthen.
- Trunk muscles strengthn.

10–12 weeks
- Gradually uncurls from fetal position.
- Posture relaxes slowly.

By 12 weeks
- Can raise head and take weight on forearms when lying on front.
- Spends much time moving arms and legs, learning muscle control.
- Has learned to lie flat and no longer holds arms and legs bent all the time.

Hand–eye coordination

10–12 weeks
- Begins to stare at hands.

By 12 weeks
- Can reach towards moving objects, not always successfully.

- Grasps objects placed in her hand, but cannot let go at will.

Senses and learning

At birth
- Has limited vision, sees best at a range of 20–25 cm (8–10 in), and squints at nearer objects.
- Blinks when light falls on her face.
- Watches mother's face intently.
- Can hear.

- Responds to sound with startle, blink or cry, depending on the sound.
- When startled her whole body reacts.

Early weeks
- Can follow dangling toy with her eyes for a moment soon after birth.

By 12 weeks
- Has learned to adjust to near vision and can see further than 25 cm (10 in).
- Can now follow moving person with her eyes.
- Makes more eye contact.
- Learns to recognize faces other than her parents'.
- Quicker at noticing objects in front of her.

- Can follow a dangling toy from one side to another.
- Can localize sound by turning her head towards the source.

Communication

At birth
- Uses whole body to express pleasure or pain.

0–2 weeks
- Makes fleeting smiling movements with mouth after a few days, but not at anyone in particular.
- Responds to parents' voices within the first few days.

By 6 weeks
- First social smile – a real smile using her whole face.

From 7 weeks
- Practises vowel sounds ('oh', 'aw'), most often in response to parent.

0–8 weeks
- Soon learns 'turn-taking' and is quiet when parent speaks, but moves and makes noises, as if actually conversing, when parent stops.

0–12 weeks
- Cries to express needs and emotions.

By 12 weeks
- Still cries for needs, but also gurgles and coos spontaneously.
- Smiles when spoken to.
- Uses facial expressions more frequently.

- Shows clear likes and dislikes: for instance, dislikes being hurried or bundled hastily from one person to another.
- Begins to demonstrate pleasure by chuckling and even laughing.
- Relishes attention and cuddles.
- May say a few consonants ('g', 'gn', 'p', 'b').

Emotions

At birth
- Is innately attached to her mother.

0–6 weeks
- Attachment deepens as mother and baby get to know each other.
- Cries become more distinctive and the repertoire broadens.

0–12 weeks
- Also forms attachments to father and other people.

By 12 weeks
- Responds positively to strangers if they are nice to her.
- May cry when upset, and now produces real tears.

Growth and health

As a new parent, you may not know what to expect. If you have never seen a newborn at close range before, let alone held your own baby in your arms, a new baby's appearance can be surprising.

Head, hair and eyes

A baby's head is large compared with his body, because the human brain is much larger than that of other species. The skull bones are still relatively soft, and there is movement between them – otherwise birth might be impossible.

Between the two halves of the skull are soft spots, called fontanelles – gaps between the bones that are still open at birth. The posterior fontanelle, towards the back, shrinks quickly and by 6 weeks you may not be able to feel it. The anterior fontanelle, at the front, enlarges before closing at around 18 months.

Some babies have a lot of scalp hair, which may stand up on end. Others have sparse, fine hair. Both are normal. The hair often changes at about 8–10 weeks, so its appearance at birth does not tell you what your baby's hair will be like later.

For the first few months, your baby's eyes are blue. However, this may not be their final colour because the iris changes slowly over the next 12–16 weeks.

Skin

At birth, your baby's tender skin may be covered with vernix. This greasy, cheesy-white substance protects him from the amniotic fluid in the womb, and it can take a few days to wear off. If your baby was born late, his skin may be dry and flaky. All this is normal.

Your baby's face may be red and wrinkled. He may also have 'stork marks'. These are purplish V-shaped marks on the back of the neck or near the eyes. He may also have a greyish blue patch (the so-called 'Mongolian blue spot') on his back or buttocks. All these are normal and fade in time.

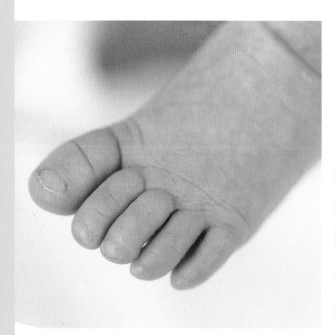

Jaundice

This yellow tinge of the skin and eyes is often seen in 2- or 3-day-old babies. The yellow colour is caused by bilirubin, a blood pigment that a new baby's liver cannot yet handle. Jaundice usually settles in about a week. If your baby has jaundice within 24 hours of birth, or if it lasts for more than 14 days, he will be given blood tests to make sure all is well.

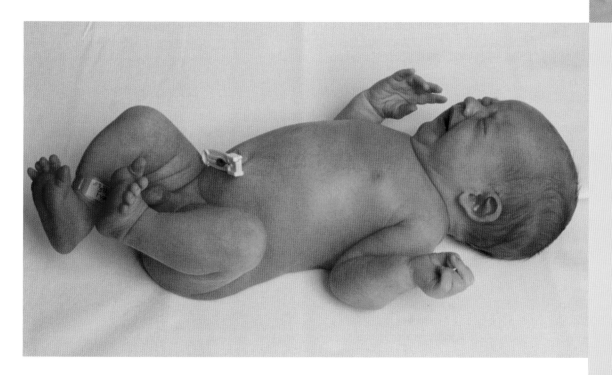

Your baby's skin may be generally blotchy. This is because the circulation is still immature at birth, so blood tends to collect in one part of the body as a result of gravity. When your baby lies on his left side, his right side may look pale. If you sit him up, something similar happens: blood pools in his legs, making them redder than his top half. This 'harlequin colour change' is normal and settles within 6 weeks as your baby's circulatory system develops.

Breasts and genitals

Enlargement of the breasts is normal in both girls and boys for a few days. It is caused by the mother's hormones and is most obvious at 7 days. Your baby may even produce a few drops of milk, but this will soon subside.

For the same reason, a newborn's genitals may look swollen. A girl may even look rather like a boy. When her hormone levels drop a week later, she may bleed a little from the vagina. This can startle new parents if they do not know about it.

Caring for the umbilical cord

In the womb, all your baby's nourishment came through his umbilical cord. After the birth, he is left with a stump of cord about 1 cm (½ in) long, to which a plastic cord clamp is attached. Within a day, the cord starts to shrivel, and the clamp falls off after about 3 days. The stump of cord usually remains until about the seventh day. A few drops of old blood may weep from the cord before it falls off but this is normal. It then heals up quickly to form a tidy and more familiar-looking belly-button (navel).

Until then, clean your baby's navel every day by gently washing it with cotton wool dipped in cooled boiled water (unless your midwife advises otherwise). If you are worried about your baby's navel, check with your midwife or health visitor.

Your baby's first medical check

If your baby is born in hospital, a paediatrician will usually give her a complete check-over. With a home delivery, your midwife or family doctor examines the baby. This is the first of several check-ups, but for many parents it is the most important as it reassures them that their baby is healthy.

Your baby's first checks

The doctor will check your baby in the following ways.

- Head shape and size: to make sure that the head shape is normal and is in correct proportion with the rest of the body.
- Eyes: to check for cataracts and other possible eye problems.
- Heart and lungs: listening with a stethoscope, to check that the heart sounds are normal and that the lungs are healthy.
- Mouth: feeling inside the mouth, to rule out problems like cleft palate.
- Abdomen and genitals: feeling around the abdomen, to check that there is no suspicion of hernia in the groin and making sure that the external genitals are normal. If your baby has not opened her

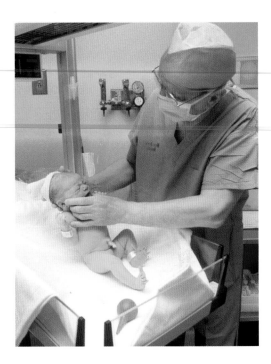

Your baby's measurements

At birth
AVERAGE WEIGHT: 3.5 kg (7 lb 11 oz)
LENGTH: about 51 cm (20 in)
HEAD CIRCUMFERENCE: about 35 cm (14 in)

At 3 months
AVERAGE WEIGHT: 5.5 kg (12 lb)
LENGTH: about 60 cm (24 in)
HEAD CIRCUMFERENCE: about 40 cm (16 in)

These measurements are only approximate and are influenced by a number of factors.

☐ Size and weight depend a lot on family history and ethnic origin.

☐ As a general rule, boys are larger and heavier than girls.

☐ Premature babies usually weigh less than average.

☐ Twins, triplets and higher multiples are often smaller than singletons. The average birth weight of a twin is 2.5 kg (5½ lb), and of a triplet about 1.8 kg (4 lb).

bowels yet, the doctor may look at the back passage.

- Spine and limbs: running a finger down your baby's spine to feel for any abnormalities, and also looking at the hands and feet.
- Hips: pressing downwards and upwards on your baby's thighs ensures that the hip joints are well developed and stable in their sockets.

At 6–8 weeks, many babies have another routine check, from either your family doctor or a paediatrician. This check includes some of the same examinations, and also tests for reflexes, muscle control and social skills.

Your baby's head shape

Young babies often have strange-looking heads. This is partly due to the effect that the actual birth itself has on your baby's soft skull bones.

Your baby's head can look lop-sided for weeks. It may even be flattened on one side. This is usually no cause for concern, although it may last a while because your baby spends a lot of time lying on her back (this can also create a temporary bald spot). Babies should sleep on their backs to reduce the risk of cot death (sudden infant death syndrome, or SIDS), so don't try to correct your baby's head shape by putting her to bed on her front. Once your baby is a few months old and is becming more mobile, her head gradually starts to become more symmetrical.

The Guthrie test

In the first 10 days, your baby will have a small blood sample taken from her heel. This is called the Guthrie test, and the blood is tested for thyroid deficiency as well as for phenyltonuria (an inborn disorder of blood chemistry). Left untreated, either of these conditions can cause lasting growth and development problems.

Interpreting growth charts

Your baby's weight, length and head circumference can be plotted on what is known as a centile chart. This is a graph on which centile curves are printed. These curves are produced by taking measurements from a large number of babies and working out what is average. There are different centile charts for boys and girls, reflecting the fact that they are not the same size.

If, for example, your baby's weight falls on the 25th percentile, it means that 75 per cent of all babies would be expected to be heavier than your baby, and 25 per cent would be lighter.

Centile charts can be a good way of monitoring a baby's growth, but they can also worry parents. The important thing to remember is that isolated results do not matter much. At this stage, steady growth is more important.

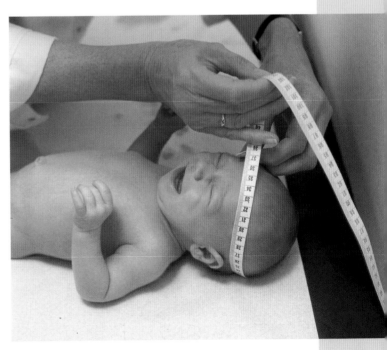

Care – feeding and sleeping

During these 3 months, your baby is growing rapidly and needs a lot of energy. Not surprisingly, his life revolves around food and rest.

Feeding

Breast milk is the ideal food, but formula milk can be nearly as good. Whichever you choose, you (and your partner) must be happy with the decision because you will spend a lot of time feeding.

Establishing a feeding routine

With your newborn, feeding seems like a 24-hour occupation. Your baby knows how to root, suck and swallow (see pages 40–43). However, his stomach is small and his digestive system is immature, so until about 4 weeks of age, he will have an erratic schedule. When he is very young, feeding on demand is usually best, but there are exceptions, especially if you have a premature baby.

Feeds are more than just fuel for the body. They also mean contact and cuddles. Each feed is an opportunity to get close to your baby, so relax and enjoy it.

Try to avoid any distractions and make eye contact as you feed. In time, you will be able to talk on the telephone, read a book or answer the door while feeding, but for the first few weeks new parents usually prefer to give their baby undivided attention.

Feeding problems

If your baby has trouble feeding, check the following possibilities.

■ He may not be hungry. Perhaps he is crying because he is tired or in pain.

■ The milk may be too hot or too cold. Check the temperature of each feed by shaking a few drops over the inside of your wrist.

■ If you are mixing breast and bottle, a baby can get 'nipple confusion' and refuse to feed from a teat. If you are planning on using both breast and bottle, introduce bottles before your baby is 4 weeks old.

■ His mouth may be sore, especially if he seems hungry then suddenly stops feeding and cries. Soreness and white spots inside his mouth may indicate thrush. Check with your doctor or health visitor.

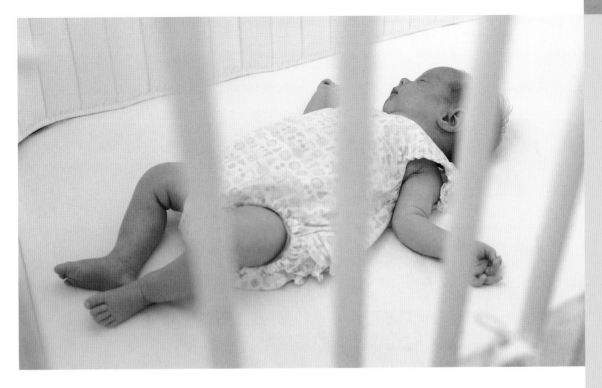

Sleeping

A baby's sleep causes new parents more problems than almost anything else.

Your baby's sleep needs

Newborn babies can sleep a lot, but many don't. It is best not to have any fixed ideas. However, there is probably some truth in the saying that babies who are very active in the womb need less sleep after they are born.

Your baby will not take all his sleep in one stretch. To begin with, his waking times are based around his feeds. Before 6 weeks, a baby may be awake for anything from 4 to 10 hours in every 24. After 6 weeks, he will be more wakeful and he will begin to distinguish daytime from night-time sleeps.

Don't worry about noise. Babies don't need quiet to nod off. However, once asleep, a sudden noise can wake a baby.

It is a good idea to get your baby used to falling asleep on his own. If you always rock your baby to sleep, he may have sleep problems later.

Safe sleeping

For at least the first 6 weeks, and preferably the first 6 months, keep your baby in your own room at night. He is still getting used to life outside the womb and needs you nearby.

- ☐ Newborn babies should sleep on their backs, to help reduce the risk of cot death.

- ☐ Keep your baby's head uncovered. Place him with his feet to the foot of the cot, so he cannot wriggle under the covers.

- ☐ Don't let your baby get too hot. The ideal room temperature is around 18 °C (65 °F).

- ☐ Cot-death experts advise against taking your baby to bed with you, especially if you or your partner smoke, have been drinking alcohol, have taken medication that makes you drowsy, or are unusually tired. It is dangerous to sleep with your baby on a sofa or armchair.

Lifting and holding your baby

Until 6 or 8 weeks of age, babies have no head control, so they are very vulnerable to injury. Consequently, you must always support your baby's head when lifting and holding her. There are many different ways to hold a baby: the best way is probably the one that comes most naturally to you.

Lifting your baby

If you or your partner are new parents, at first you may need to make a conscious effort to support both your baby's head and her body. This is the way to do it.

- Put one hand under your baby's head and neck, and the other under her bottom.

- Lift her slowly, always keeping her close to your body.
- Turn her towards your chest. If you are bending down, straighten your body at the same time.

Holding your baby

You can hold a baby comfortably in various different positions. If she is awake, she will probably be happiest if she can see your face at all times.

Research shows that babies also prefer to be held in their parent's left arm. Many mothers do this instinctively, and it has the benefit of leaving your right hand relatively free, a bonus for the right-handed. It also means that your baby can hear and feel your heart beat, which may be why babies like it.

There are various ways of holding your baby. Whichever position you choose, look where you're going when carrying your baby.

- You can hold her on your arm facing you, using the crook of your left elbow to support her head and your right hand to support her bottom.
- You can hold her against your shoulder. For the first few months, use one hand to support her head as well.
- Some babies enjoy lying face down on a forearm. One of your arms can support her head and chest, and the other hand can stabilize her lower body. She will not be able to see much of you, but she will get a view of the floor, which she may enjoy if you walk about while holding her. This can also be a good position for babies with wind or colic.

Gaining confidence

Try to relax. Put your baby at ease by smiling and talking to her as you pick her up or hold her. Take things slowly. There is rarely any need to rush to pick her up, or to hand her over quickly to someone else. Hasty movements seem rough to a baby and may even make her cry.

New fathers may feel clumsy with their new baby, but they quickly become more confident. The most important things are to support the head and not to hurry. Letting father look after the baby is good for your baby and the whole family.

You will soon get used to doing simple household chores while holding your baby.

Of course, you cannot do everything with a baby in one arm, so prioritize ruthlessly. Leave some tasks until your baby is asleep, or abandon them altogether.

Using a sling

A sling helps free your hands and keeps your baby close. There are several different types, and many have a head-piece to support your baby's head in the first few weeks. You can usually detach this later, giving your baby better all-round visibility. As she grows heavier, carrying her in a sling may hurt your back, in which case use it for short periods only. Getting your baby in and out of the sling is another consideration – choose a model that is comfortable and easy to use.

A sling is a good way of taking a walk with your baby when you don't want to use a pram or buggy. It is certainly better than simply holding your baby. Carrying a baby in your arms while you walk down the street can be dangerous, especially if the pavements are crowded or it is dark.

Babies usually enjoy being in a sling, but may not want to stay in one for long. Don't be surprised if, to begin with, your baby gets fidgety after half an hour or so.

Motor development

Although your newborn now has more space to move and stretch than when he was in the womb, he still lies curled up a lot of the time, with his back rounded, his arms and legs bent, and his fists clenched.

Body

At first, your baby's muscles are weak, but during his waking hours he busies himself by exercising his arms and legs. When he kicks, one leg often goes up while the other goes down, as if he is riding a bicycle. Over the next 10–12 weeks his muscles get stronger, enabling his body to unfold gently. By 12 weeks, if you put him on his front, his pelvis lies flat and his legs turn outwards like a frog.

Head

At birth, your baby has a short neck and no head control. If you hold him up on his front, his head lolls.

A few weeks later, it is a very different story. By 12 weeks, when lying on his back, your baby can move his head to watch whatever attracts his attention. When he lies on his front, he can now raise his head and hold it there for several minutes at a time. If you pull him up gently to a sitting position, his head lolls only slightly.

Once your baby is upright, he is able to balance his head momentarily. He can even turn his head, although you have to hold him in support because he does not yet have the knack of controlling his upper trunk as he does so.

Hand–eye coordination

At birth, hand–eye coordination is almost non-existent, as if your baby does not know yet what hands are for. He may suck his thumb, but that is about all.

His fists gradually become less tightly gripped. By 12 weeks, his hands lie open, ready to touch and explore the world around him. Using his whole fist, he can grasp an object placed in his hand. However, at this stage his hold is partly involuntary and after a few seconds he lets go without realizing it. He cannot move his hand while he is holding anything, so rattles are not much use to him until he is about 4 months of age.

At around 12 weeks, your baby discovers his hands. He watches them move and waves them in front of his eyes. He also puts them into his mouth. At this age, hands and mouth were made for each other, and discovering the relationship between the two is an important phase of his learning.

Stimulating your baby's motor development

Your baby's first and most fascinating toy is you.

- Let your baby explore your face. He will enjoy looking at and smelling your skin and hair, as well as touching them. If you wear spectacles, take them off first.

- If your baby uses a dummy, leave it out of his mouth as much as you can. Dummies can be useful for soothing fractious babies, but they stop them experimenting with their hands and mouth.

- Let your baby experience different positions. He can be on his front for playtime, although not for sleep. Sometimes he will enjoy being in a bouncy chair, but he will not want to be in one place for very long at a time. At this stage, it is up to you to move him before he gets tired or bored.

- Your baby is never too young for songs and nursery rhymes. He will love being bounced gently on your lap. This gives him a chance to use his trunk and limb muscles, as well as to enjoy new sound experiences while still feeling secure with you. Be gentle, as he is not ready for anything rough or too new.

- You can massage your baby anytime from 2 weeks onwards. It is a lovely way of showing your love. Massage is also soothing and may help tone his muscles and boost his immune system. Massage from the head downwards, starting with his front. Work his wrists and hands, gently stroking each finger with your fingertips and thumb. Stroke his legs downwards, from thighs to knees, and from knees right down to his toes. Give each tiny toe gentle individual attention.

Your baby's early reflexes

Your newborn baby comes equipped with a bundle of reflex actions. A few are vital to her survival, but others are of less obvious use. Some, such as the grasp reflex, are an evolutionary reminder of our primitive past. These early reflexes disappear as your baby's brain develops and her movements come under voluntary control.

Sucking

This is one of your baby's most basic reflexes. She even practised it in the womb. Now she sucks any vaguely nipple-like shape put into her mouth, whether it is a rubber teat or your fingertip.

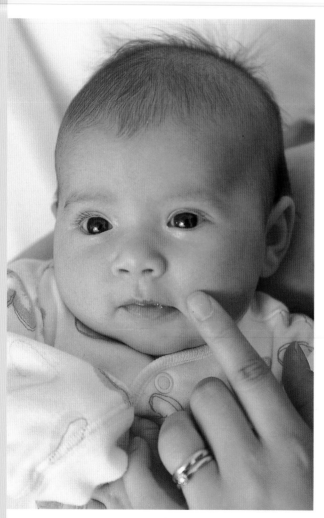

Swallowing

Another reflex action at this age is swallowing. Again, it is something babies do before birth when they swallow amniotic fluid in the womb.

Rooting

Turning the head and mouth when the side of the cheek is stroked is known as rooting. Your baby therefore moves towards the nipple when it touches her face, which is obviously useful for finding the breast and starting to feed.

Some reflexes are simpler than others. The rooting reflex is complicated because it is actually made up of several different components. When you touch a corner of your baby's mouth, she lowers her bottom lip on that side and moves her tongue towards the corner. If you slide your finger sideways across her face, she will turn her whole head to follow it. In the same way, if you touch the middle of her lower lip, she will lift the lip.

Sneezing

This is also a reflex action, which explains why young babies sneeze so much. Your baby automatically sneezes if her nose is irritated in any way, or even if the light is bright.

Blinking

When you shine a light or touch your baby's head, whether or not she is awake, she will blink. Together with sneezing, this is probably a protective reflex.

The startle reflex

Sudden noise or movement triggers the startle reflex. Until about 8 weeks, your baby responds by throwing out her arms and legs, then closing them again. You may see this reflex if you accidentally nudge your baby's pram or rocking chair.

The stepping or walking reflex

This reflex is a series of step-like movements that a baby makes when the sole of her foot meets a firm surface. It disappears within 3 or 4 weeks, so it is usually there at your baby's first examination, and gone when she is checked 6 weeks later.

The grasp reflex

The grasp reflex is very strong in newborn babies. If you put anything in the palm of her hand, your baby will automatically grip it tight. The grasp reflex usually disappears by about 4 weeks, but until then it is so reliable that you could even pull your baby up just by one finger placed in her hand. For a baby ape, this is probably a good way of clinging onto its mother's fur and staying safe, and this may explain why human babies also have this reflex. There is even a grasp reflex in the foot of a newborn baby, but this also disappears altogether by around 8 weeks.

Practical matters

A baby's early reflexes fade as her nervous system matures. Therefore, persistence of any of these reflexes can be significant. This is why doctors sometimes check to see if they are still present at about 4 weeks. However, in itself persistence of a reflex is seldom a sign of anything serious. Nobody would diagnose a problem such as cerebral palsy, for example, without a clutch of other major symptoms being present.

Nowadays, doctors are much less keen on testing reflexes. It is also a waste of time for a parent to deliberately look for their baby's reflexes and could also annoy your baby. However, knowing about reflexes can help a parent to understand the course of their baby's development.

The fact that the reflexes exist at all in humans is interesting, as it reflects our species' ancestry. One curious fact is that some of the reflexes can appear later in life, for example in people with senile dementia, or in those who have had a stroke. In both these cases, movements are not under voluntary control, just as in a young baby.

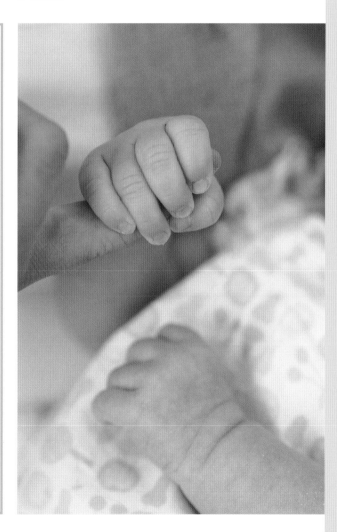

Senses and learning

Your baby's abilities may seem limited at birth, but he has all five senses to help him take in his surroundings. His senses develop quickly, and he soon learns new things.

Vision

At birth, your baby has good vision up to a distance of 20–25 cm (8–10 in). This just happens to be how far away your face is, so it is ideal for getting to know you.

Your baby's brain already knows what is important. At the back of the brain, an area called the occipital cortex processes the

information from his eyes. Your baby already recognizes patterns, especially human faces. Research shows that new babies are more interested in looking at a sketch of a face than at a card with a random pattern. They also prefer smiling faces to grumpy ones.

At birth, your baby's eye muscles are uncoordinated, so he has trouble focusing on near objects and may squint when he tries to do so. Because he cannot see distant objects, they hold little interest for him. For the first 12 weeks, his world is what is close by. He studies you intently, blinking only when light falls on his face.

A baby's vision gradually develops. By 12 weeks he is better at near vision and he squints less. He also sees further than 25 cm (10 in), so he can follow a moving person more easily. Now his brain is maturing rapidly, with huge numbers of new connections between cells. What he sees becomes more meaningful. He is quicker at spotting what is in front of him, and he can follow a dangling toy from one side to another. Different faces are more significant to him.

Hearing

Your baby has acute hearing at birth, and he recognizes the sounds he heard in the womb. He knows your voice as well as some of the music you listened to before he was born. Even newborns shows more interest in human speech than in other sounds. Your baby reacts to loud or sudden noise, sometimes violently. This tells you that you must protect him, as he cannot move for himself yet.

Helping your baby to use his senses

From the moment he is born, you can help your baby make the most of his senses.

- Let him see what is around him. From time to time, he may like sitting on your lap facing outwards.

- Prams with high sides are safe but dull. Consider putting a picture or a toy or two inside the pram.

- When your baby is in a sling, try not to block his view. He will usually be happiest with his head turned to one side, so he can see.

- Let him hear music, but don't play it too loudly. Noise can damage the hearing permanently.

- If he is fractious, the sound of your voice will soothe him. White noise or a 'womb tape' can work too, but your baby needs to get used to it within 2 weeks of birth.

- Allow your baby to feel what is around him. Mittens are good in the cold, but they interfere with his sense of touch.

By 12 weeks his ears are more attuned and he can localize sound better. He now turns his head towards a noise.

Taste and smell

Even at birth, a baby prefers the smell of his mother to anything else. Your baby does not have to learn your smell, or the taste of your milk.

Both taste and smell develop further with time. It will be a while before your baby needs to try out different foods, but if you are breast-feeding he is already familiar with traces of the things that you eat. This perhaps helps later when he starts to share family meals.

Touch

Your baby makes sense of his world using touch just as much as his other senses. Crammed into your baby's skin is a rich network of sensory nerve endings to help him detect sensations such as touch, pressure, pain, a tickle, heat, cold and vibration. All these are essential for your baby's immediate survival and for his future learning. Even at birth, he likes things that feel soft. At about 12 weeks, his hands become a major tool for exploring. His thin skin, exquisitely sensitive to touch, makes his fingers just perfect for experimenting with and for finding out what he likes and what he doesn't like.

Toys

The shops are full of tempting toys. In the first few weeks, new parents often want to get their new baby lots of cute playthings. Choosing these is all part of the fun of having a baby. You will no doubt also receive some toys as gifts. Playing is an essential part of your baby's development. Toys stimulate the senses, help your baby to learn and enable her to practise new skills.

Choosing toys

Even when they are beautifully made, not all toys are equally good. In the first 12 weeks, a variety of simple toys is best. You can gradually build up a toy box that sustains your baby's interests and helps her discover new ones.

Soft toys

Babies love dolls, teddy bears and other furry animals. They enjoy looking at the faces as well as exploring the different textures.

Toys that make a noise

Rattles, chiming balls and squeaky toys often fascinate babies. At first your baby will not be able to make the noise herself, but she will like it when you shake the rattle or squeeze the noisy animal for her.

Mobiles

Babies love mobiles. Anything brightly coloured appeals to them, as do contrasting patterns. Babies are intrigued by mobiles with faces, animals or dolls.

Baby gym

In the first few weeks, when your baby has little hand–eye coordination, a baby gym or activity centre will probably interest her mainly because it is nice to look at.

Mirrors

A mirror could be your baby's first interactive toy. There are unbreakable ones to be attached to the inside of a cot or playpen.

There is such a thing as too many toys. Your baby can get bored or overwhelmed in the midst of plenty, and may cry if she is surrounded by lots of playthings. Sometimes all she wants is a quiet cuddle from you.

Games to stimulate the senses

It is fun to get your baby to copy your expressions. Even a very young baby quickly learns to poke her tongue in and out in response to you.

Use songs and nursery rhymes. You can play 'This Little Piggy' or 'Round and Round the Garden' from an early age. She will enjoy being touched as she hears the rhyme, and before long she will anticipate what happens next.

Your baby may enjoy her tummy and feet being splashed while you bathe her. You need to hold her very securely and only play splashing games if she enjoys bathtime. Some babies take a month or two to develop a liking for bathing.

Safety first

Keep your baby safe by taking the following precautions.

☐ Choose toys that are appropriate for your baby's age and make sure that there are no loose parts that could injure her or make her choke.

☐ Check that any eyes, buttons and the like are firmly attached to soft toys.

☐ Remove ribbons from teddies and soft toys so that your baby does not swallow them.

☐ Don't use ribbon or string to secure toys to the buggy, or else keep it very short. A length of ribbon can strangle a baby.

☐ Clean toys occasionally by wiping them with antiseptic solution. Plastic toys can often be soaked or put into the dishwasher. You should also clean second-hand toys before giving them to your baby.

☐ Loud noise damages young ears and the effect is cumulative, so don't put noisy toys near your baby for long periods of time. For the first few months, a baby cannot move away by herself. You need to be aware of noise as well as other hazards.

☐ If you have an older child, many of his playthings will be unsuitable or even dangerous for a baby, so encourage him to keep his toys away from the baby.

Communication

Right from the start, your baby communicates, although he cannot say a word. He picks up subtle clues from your tone of voice, your face and your gestures in order to gradually work out what you are saying. By way of reply, he uses his own body language and basic noises.

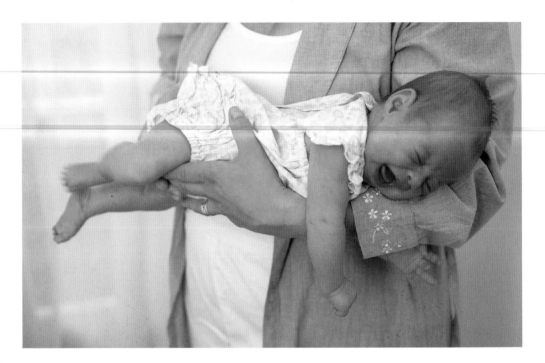

Crying

In the first 6 weeks or so, a baby uses crying as the main way of expressing himself. Interminable crying can be extremely wearing for new parents, but it is very effective because you are programmed to respond to it.

Your baby uses body language too, such as curling up or stretching. Then there are facial expressions, like blinking and grimacing, which become more and more eloquent as time passes. Within about 4 weeks of birth, he uses his whole body to maximum effect. The aim is for you to respond accordingly – and it works very effectively!

Smiling

Your baby makes his first proper smile at about 6 weeks. Before this, babies make many smile-like expressions. Some are fleeting, and you may think they are simply 'wind'. In fact they are smiles, in the sense that your baby is deliberately moving his facial muscles. At around 6 weeks, however, you will see a real smile because your baby's eyes will light up as well. If you then smile back, his smile gets even broader, and he will look delighted.

Nobody is sure exactly what makes a baby begin to smile. Your facial expressions help, but it does not wholly depend on them because blind babies smile too.

Talking to your baby

Parents instinctively talk to their baby at a higher pitch, and they simplify what they say. Baby talk is useful at this stage because it helps a baby to learn the different sounds within speech. Babies also like the soft cooing sounds and the exaggerated tones.

Talking back to you

Your baby will move his mouth in response to you. By 8 weeks, he is really interacting. Babies learn by imitation right from the start, and he will soon be making his own little sounds back at you.

He times much of this for the lulls in your speaking. In other words, you both take turns. This is apparent in babies just a few days old and gradually becomes more obvious. When you speak, your baby keeps still and listens. When you stop, he makes sounds and moves his body. If you don't respond, he may become puzzled or distressed, and he may cry.

Pre-speaking skills

Even in the first 12 weeks, your baby can pick up meaningful sounds. This ability to learn language is innate. He learns by example too, so the more you talk to him the better it is for his language development. It will be some time before he can reply properly, but this does not matter. 'Receptive language' is always ahead of 'expressive language'. In other words, babies understand before they can speak.

First sounds

Your baby's first sounds are all vowel sounds, such as 'ah', 'eh', 'uh' and 'oh', which he usually starts making in earnest from about 7 weeks onwards.

Although he makes various sounds, he may prefer just one or two ('oh' is often one of his favourites). He also coos with pleasure.

By 12 weeks, he may say a couple of consonants. He uses 'g' and 'gn' mostly when he is content, but 'p' and 'b' are the sounds that he might make when he is fretful.

Communicating with your baby

Take every opportunity to communicate with your baby.

- Spend time with him. The chores can wait. Interacting with your baby is wonderful for his language skills and rewarding for you.

- Make eye contact when you are together. This is important for learning words and their meaning.

- Nappy-changing, feeding, bathing and the rest of the baby routine are all chances to speak to your baby on a one-to-one basis.

- Keep background noise down when speaking to your baby.

- React to the sounds your baby makes.

- Use his name, so that he gets to know it.

- Songs and nursery rhymes help a baby learn speech patterns – and he will not mind if you are tone-deaf!

Emotions

In your baby's first 12 weeks, everyone's emotions are very near the surface. This is normal and soon passes, leading to more settled times.

Relationship with you

As far as relationships are concerned, you are initially the most important person in her life.

The emotional connection that forms between parents and their baby is known as 'bonding'. This two-way process develops as you and your baby become closer and more inextricably linked. It can start before birth. Many mothers claim to feel a deep passion from the first scan or their baby's first kicks.

For other mothers, positive feelings come later. Some do not bond with their baby until after the birth. Even then it can take many days, especially after a difficult labour. Most of these mothers bond eventually, but if you have concerns speak to your midwife, health visitor or family doctor.

Relationships with other people

As the weeks pass, your baby's attention and affection expands to include others. By 12 weeks, she can respond positively to her other carers. She also smiles at strangers who are nice to her.

Crying

Babies cry to express moods and feelings. Your baby cries when she is hungry, cold, hot or uncomfortable, or in pain, lonely, bored, tired, afraid, overwhelmed or wants a cuddle. However, she seldom produces any tears until about 12 weeks, when her tear ducts mature.

You will soon recognize subtle differences in her cries. A cry of pain is often loud and piercing. A cry of hunger varies in pitch. A grumbling cry can mean tiredness or irritability.

You may worry about giving your baby too much attention, but babies cry for a reason, and you are right to respond. As the weeks pass, she sometimes makes a short 'testing' cry when, for instance, you put her in the cot. Wait a minute if she only makes a tiny whimper, but investigate anything more than this.

Some babies cry more than others, and it is not always possible to pre-empt it, or even to understand the cause.

• If your baby is fed and comfortable, she may be over-stimulated. Put her in the cot to see if she dozes off.

- Take her out in the buggy or pram. She may still cry, but the noise seems less loud outside.
- Leave her with your partner or another responsible adult and unwind for half an hour.
- If you cannot cope with constant crying, ask your health visitor or a close friend for help.

Body language

As the weeks pass, your baby will develop a range of facial expressions to convey how she feels. She soon uses her whole body too. There is no mistaking what pleases her, be it attention, a cuddle or a favourite toy. When she is excited, she kicks about. If she is agitated, her movements are violent and she moves her head from side to side.

How to reduce crying

There are a number of ways to reduce your baby's crying.

- Try to relax. Babies instinctively know when you are tense.
- Remember that you are the expert on your baby (or soon will be).
- Establish a comfortable routine. Babies like predictability.
- Don't let your baby cry too long for a feed. She may become distressed and swallow a lot of air with the feed, leading to more crying later.

Bonding

There are many myths about bonding that can worry parents.

Myth You have to breast-feed to bond.
Fact No research has ever proven this. It is pointless and illogical to feel guilty if you decide to bottle-feed. Hugs, by contrast, are absolutely essential.

Myth You must hold your baby close immediately after birth.
Fact It is lovely to have your newborn placed on your chest or belly right away, but this may not always be possible, and it is not essential for bonding.

Myth If you don't feel an immediate love at the birth, you will not bond.
Fact Many mothers (and fathers) feel an overwhelming rush of love for their baby as soon as she is born, but it is not essential. It can take time to get to know your baby.

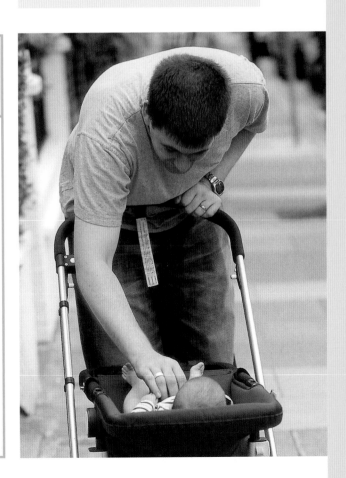

3–6 months

Reaching out

Major milestones

- ✔ Eyes reach their final colour
- ✔ Starts on solid foods
- ✔ Sleeps through the night
- ✔ Develops better head control
- ✔ Rolls from side to side
- ✔ Sits up
- ✔ Grasps objects
- ✔ Reaches for objects
- ✔ Puts toes in mouth

Things to look out for

From 3 to 6 months is the time when your baby starts getting to grips with his world. He is not mobile yet, but he is discovering his hands. At first he studies them, as if working out what they are for. Soon he will be reaching for everything in sight. He grabs clumsily at first, but his accuracy improves almost daily.

Physical changes

Your baby undergoes a lot of physical changes in these 3 months. His toothless gums may soon sprout first one small tooth, followed by its neighbour. He may be drooling, as well as gnawing whatever is available to soothe his sore gums.

Now that your baby's body is stronger, his coordination is far better. He can roll from front to back, so he can change position without your help. When you carry him, you can feel his extra strength as well as his increasing weight. He tries to sit up, but until he is able to do so he likes being propped up on pillows. He enjoys seeing the world the right way up, although it may still be a while before he can support himself in an upright position.

Safety now becomes an important issue, because once your baby can roll, he can also fall off a surface and hurt himself. From now on, you need to anticipate his next stage of development and think ahead to keep him safe.

Your baby and his environment

Your baby observes everything closely. Now he rarely squints when paying attention to detail. As an aid to exploration, he uses his mouth to work out taste and texture. Whatever fits into his mouth, goes in. He also makes valiant attempts to chew or suck objects that are far too large for his mouth. Sucking his feet gives him huge pleasure.

During these 3 months, your baby also reaches out to other people. He becomes hugely sociable. He smiles freely, bestowing his own dazzling look on anyone who is nice to him. He gurgles and giggles with pleasure. When he is happy, he shows this with his whole body, and he may rock back and forth with excitement. He is secure in your love, so strangers are no threat to him yet.

Your baby may soon be sleeping through the night. If not, he is well on the way to learning the difference between night and day, which may come as a relief to most parents.

At some time between 4 and 6 months of age, your baby may have his first taste of solid foods. He will like some but not others. This too is a measure of the acuteness of his senses.

Communicating

Your baby's hearing is good, and he turns towards sounds. He can hear a dog bark in the garden or a lorry passing outside. He knows the sound of the key in the door as soon as you or your partner come in, and he gets excited before he sees the person he longs for.

His communication skills come on apace. He understands more and more every day, and his vocabularies of sounds and facial expressions are increasing. He babbles to himself, especially when he is content, and he becomes positively chatty with you. All in all, he is great company, and you will be sharing many happy conversations, although your baby produces no real words yet.

This is a sunny time, but you cannot expect it to be all smiles. As your baby's personality gradually emerges, he lets you know his likes and dislikes. He kicks out with growing strength if you don't meet his needs, or if he feels frustrated.

Child care

A welcome routine has taken the place of the muddle of the early weeks. By now, most new parents have adapted well and revel in this happy phase of babyhood. About now, you may be starting to think about returning to work. Arranging child care can cause some concerns, but babies quickly get used to a new face. Indeed, having another adult to care for your baby can actively enrich his life and stimulate his ongoing development.

Summary of development

Growth and health

By 3 months
- Circulation maturing, but temperature control is still quite poor.
- Skin is smooth and soft.

From 3 months
- Her body grows rapidly, more so than her head.

3–4 months
- Becomes more coordinated.

By 4 months
- Rarely squints.
- Eyes reach their final colour.

4–5 months
- Any flat areas on the skull should even out.

5–6 months
- May dribble copiously as a prelude to teething.

Care

From 3 months
- Begins to distinguish between night and day.

By 4 months
- May be still on milk only, or having small tastes of baby rice (see page 58).
- Appetite may increase with rising nutritional needs.

4–6 months
- May be weaned onto solid food but milk remains the main food.

By 5 months
- May be having two meals of solids a day.

By 6 months
- Will need solids if she has not already started them.
- May start sleeping through the night.

Motor development

From 3 months
- Arm and leg movements become more purposeful.
- Can change her position more often.

By 4 months
- Head control is good.

From about 4 months
- Can roll from back to side, and side to back.
- Can sit up if held.
- Can sit unaided if her lower back is supported.

By 5 months
- Wriggles when held on lap or in arms.
- Uses hands to prop herself up when sitting.
- Takes weight on her elbows when lying on her front and leans on one arm to free the other for reaching a toy.
- May be able to roll onto front (the most difficult rolling movement).

By 6 months
- May pivot whole body when lying on the floor in preparation for moving by creeping.
- May anticipate being lifted up by holding up her arms or head.
- May sit unsupported for a short time.

Hand–eye coordination

By 3 months
- Reaches out but may miss her target.

From 3 months
- Plays with fingers.

By 4 months
- Can hold a rattle.

By 5 months
- Can keep a rattle or small toy in her hand for several minutes but often drops them accidentally.

By 6 months
- Can reach out more accurately.

Senses and learning

By about 3 months
- Puts most things into her mouth.
- Can anticipate pleasant events, such as bathtime.

From 3 months
- Visual horizons expand as eye muscles develop and both near and distant vision improves.

- Can focus more easily on objects close to her.
- Acutely aware of sounds, especially speech.
- Sound localization more accurate and begins to notice more distant sounds.
- Has a better understanding of the significance of various sounds.
- Touch very important as she reaches out for objects and handles them to find out more about the world.
- Lips and tongue are very sensitive and she puts objects into her mouth for taste, texture and temperature.

At 3–4 months
- Stares at strangers with fascination.

From 4 months
- May examine objects for a long time.
- Can follow objects through 180 degrees with her head.
- Taste and smell developing fast, especially after first experiments with solid foods.

By 6 months
- May bang things on floor or table to make a noise.

Communication

By 3 months
- Still makes mostly single-syllable vowel sounds.

From 3 months
- Babbles, coos and makes facial expressions.

By about 4 months
- May say 'ah-goo'.
- Chuckles at simple games like 'peek-a-boo'.

By 6 months
- May say 'ba' or 'da'.

Emotions

By 3 months
- Enjoys company.
- Has become attached to one or more persons.

By 3 months
- Shows excitement and frustration.
- Uses her whole body to convey emotions.

From 3 months
- Enters a very sociable phase.
- Very responsive to parents speaking and smiling.

3–4 months
- May smile less at strangers.

By 6 months
- May be shy with strangers.

Growth and health

Your baby is growing fast now, as well as changing subtly in shape. His trunk is filling out and getting sturdier, and his arms and legs look less diminutive. By 5 months, he may have doubled his birth weight. Hair and nails are growing rapidly too. It will be a long time before he needs a haircut, but his nails need frequent trimming.

Head, teeth and eyes

Any early flat areas on his skull should have evened out by about 4 or 5 months, because your baby is no longer lying on his back in one position all the time, as he did in his first 3 months. When awake, he spends more of his time on his front, kicking his arms and legs.

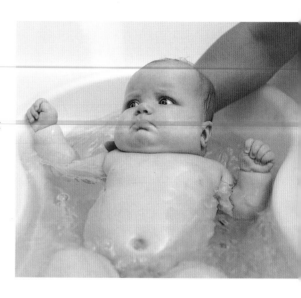

From about the fifth month, your baby may dribble and drool a lot as a prelude to his first tooth coming through. This first tooth will be one of the bottom middle incisors. Your baby will now chew on anything he can find, especially hard objects, because it soothes his sore gums (see also pages 80–81).

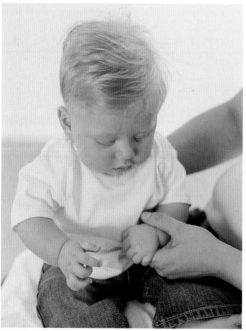

Your baby's measurements

At 3 months
AVERAGE WEIGHT: 5.5 kg (12 lb)
LENGTH: about 60 cm (24 in)
HEAD CIRCUMFERENCE: about 40 cm (16 in)

At 6 months
AVERAGE WEIGHT: 7.3 kg (16 lb)
LENGTH: about 65 cm (26 in)
HEAD CIRCUMFERENCE: about 43 cm (17 in)

These figures are only approximate, so don't worry if your baby's measurements don't tally exactly. Boys tend to be larger and heavier than girls. Family build is important too. What really matters is that your baby makes steady progress at a rate that is right for him.

Your baby's eyes will reach their final colour at about 4 months. This is often a time when family resemblances are debated in earnest. Squinting should now be rare because his eye muscles are stronger. If your baby still squints at 4 or 5 months, see your family doctor without delay. Squints sometimes run in families. If this applies to your baby, you should take any hint of a squint even more seriously and get prompt advice.

Skin

By 3 months, your baby's skin should be smooth and soft – the proverbial perfect baby skin. His circulation has developed, but he is still not very good at controlling his body temperature. You need to dress him appropriately so that he gets neither too hot nor too cold.

Some common skin conditions occur in this age group nonetheless. Strawberry marks (also known as capillary haemangioma) are common, and your baby may have one or more of these. These so-called 'birthmarks' are red and raised like a strawberry, but they actually appear after birth and grow to reach their maximum size about the age of 5 or 6 months. Almost all of them fade in time, starting from the centre, and disappear by the age of 5 years. However, if your baby has a large one in an awkward place, for instance near the eye, then laser treatment is an option.

Eczema

Eczema is a dry, scaly skin condition that often appears when a baby is about 5 months old, usually on the cheeks, trunk, and sometimes the limbs. It can look inflamed, and your baby may find it itchy. Emollients help control it.

Eczema is linked to asthma and other allergies, but not always. Because eczema can start at about the time of weaning, it is often attributed to a food allergy. In fact, food allergies rarely cause eczema, so don't restrict your baby's feeds without speaking to your doctor.

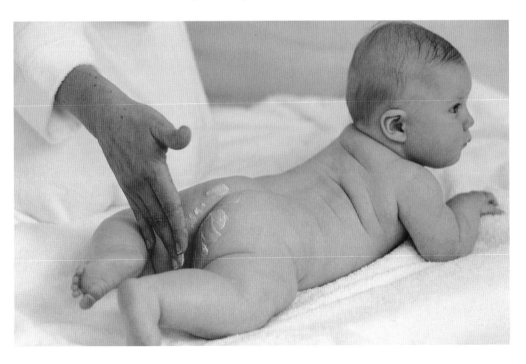

Care – feeding and sleeping

As your baby settles into a more regular pattern of feeding and sleeping, you should find life easier.

Feeding

During these 3 months, your baby's growth continues apace. She will be taking more and more milk, and by about 6 months you may think of starting her on solid foods.

When to start solid foods

Four months used to be the age advised for weaning a baby onto solid food, but recent recommendations from the World Health Organization mean that many countries have revised their advice. Parents may now be told to wait until 6 months before giving their baby solids.

However, there is debate about this. Many experts believe 4 months may be the better time in developed countries, where infectious diarrhoea is less of a threat, and where babies are usually bigger and so have greater nutritional needs. If you put off weaning until 6 months, your baby may get very hungry once milk no longer satisfies him. Therefore most mothers in the UK still choose to wean their baby between about 4 months and 6 months. On the other hand, don't introduce solids before 17 weeks because your baby's digestive system and kidneys won't be ready for them.

What to give and when

From 17 weeks onwards, if you decide to start, try giving your baby small amounts of baby rice once a day. This is bland and unlikely to cause allergies. You can mix the rice with breast milk, formula or cooled boiled water.

Drinks

Your baby still needs breast milk, infant formula or follow-on milk. Cows' milk should not be her main drink until she is 1 year old. She also needs fluids, such as water and baby juices.

By 5 months, she should begin to use a cup rather than a bottle for all her drinks except breast milk. Try a trainer beaker first.

Is your baby ready for solids?

There are a number of indications that your baby may be ready for solids.

- After previously sleeping through the night, your baby starts waking again in the night for feeds.

- Breast or bottle feeds may no longer satisfy her hunger.

- Your baby's weight gain may level off.

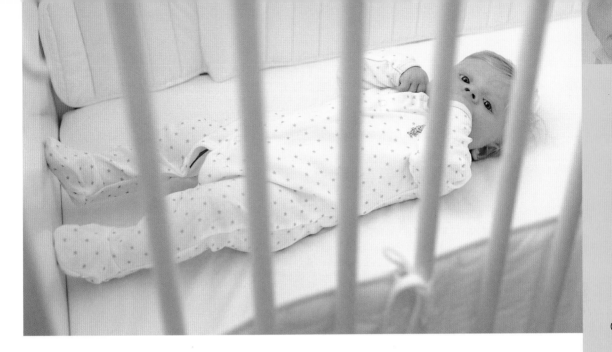

The small holes make the change from bottle to cup much easier.

Sleeping

By 3 months, you will have established a routine for you and your baby. She is now far more aware of her surroundings and attuned to the rhythms of daily activities. This means that she is also aware of important differences between day and night.

Helping your baby to sleep

If she is not yet sleeping through the night, she probably will be by about 6 months, so stay as relaxed as you can. There are several steps you can take to encourage your baby's sleeping.

- Keep night-time disturbances to a minimum.
- If you have to change or feed her at night-time, speak softly or not at all.
- Keep the lights low.
- Make the whole experience as unexciting as possible. This will encourage her to fall asleep again.
- Thick curtains at the window can keep out bright early-morning light.

Safe sleeping

At 3–6 months, you should still put your baby to sleep on her back. Continue to follow the safe sleeping advice to prevent cot death (see page 35). Your baby is too young for either a duvet or a pillow yet. However, she is growing, and soon she will be rolling over at night. Once she can roll over, you don't have to worry about her sleeping position.

- Don't rock your baby to sleep, even if you did this when she was a new born. She has to learn to doze off on her own.

Don't worry if she stirs in the night. This does not mean that she needs anything. Adults take about 90 minutes to go from being awake to deep sleep and then to being awake again. In babies aged 6 months, the awake-sleep-awake cycle takes more like 45 minutes, so your baby will wake many times in the night. If she is still sharing your room, as most babies are until 6 months of age, you may be aware of her wakeful moments, but unless she cries, no action is needed.

Motor development

Your baby's increasing size and strength now make him capable of much more. He becomes more active, especially from about 5 months. It is as if he cannot wait to practise all the new movements that he has learned.

Head

His head control is now much better. From about 3 months, there is no need to support his head when you carry him, unless he is asleep.

When your baby lies on his front, he holds his head up to get a good view. If he is on his back, he tends to keep his head in the midline, until something interesting (such as you or a toy) grabs his attention. This is why the early asymmetry of his skull has now almost gone.

At 4 months, your baby's head hardly wobbles at all when you hold him and carry him. By 5 months, if you pull him into a sitting position, there is no trace at all of the head lag that was seen in the earlier months. Your baby's head control is now perfect, just in time for his really active phase.

Rolling

At 4 months, your baby is so strong that he can now begin to roll. He rolls first from back to side and side to back. He usually kicks while he is doing this.

At 5 months, he moves his trunk a lot, changing position from lying flat on his front to pushing up on his arms. This kind of movement is useful for rolling.

From 5 months onwards, your baby may be able to roll from his back or side onto his front, which is the most challenging roll.

Sitting up

Sitting up is an important development. It means your baby can see the world the right way up, just like you.

Helping your baby's muscle control

There are a number of things you can do to improve your baby's muscle control.

- Bouncing games and nursery rhymes help his balance and muscle control, and he will enjoy them too.

- Your baby is very physical now and may enjoy a large teddy to hug.

- At about 5 or 6 months, he is ready to graduate from his baby bath to a full-size bath, which gives him more scope for splashing and kicking. To begin with, you can put the baby bath inside the adult bath-tub, which will help him get used to it (and save water). Make sure you hold him securely at all times.

At 3–4 months, your baby enjoys sitting if you hold him. His back is no longer rounded, except for its very lowest part. By 4 months, he may even sit unaided when you support his lower back.

By 5 months, he is more stable. When he is sitting on your lap, he may wriggle to adjust his position. When he is sitting on the floor, he will use his hands to prop himself up.

Your 6-month-old baby still cannot get into a sitting position on his own, but he anticipates being pulled up, and he holds his hands out for you to grasp. Now when he is sitting up, his back is totally straight. If you tilt him from side to side, he can readjust the balance of his head and trunk.

Preparing for more action

From about 5 months, your baby becomes very active and flexible. At 5 months, he may put his toes in his mouth to suck them. When he is lying on his front, he moves a lot. A favourite pose is the 'airplane', when he lifts his arms and legs off the floor and holds them aloft.

At 5 months, your baby discovers that he can lean on one arm, thereby freeing the other hand for reaching out for a toy. It is fascinating to watch just how purposeful he can be. On his front, he can also move around in a circle, by pivoting or pushing with his arms. This is a sign that he will soon learn how to creep. From there it is only a short step until he is crawling properly.

Hand–eye coordination

This is your baby's reaching out phase. She is not mobile yet, but she starts getting her hands on everything she can. As a result, her hand–eye coordination improves all the time.

Hands and eyes together

At about 3 months, your baby's brain is making better connections, so she can begin to link what she sees with what she does. She can now also focus at closer range, and her hands no longer lie tightly shut all the time. This is why, from about now, your baby enters a stage sometimes called 'hand regard'. While lying on her back or her side, she will spend a lot of time gazing at her fingers, waving them about in front of her face and watching her fist open and closed. This is the run-up to doing really interesting things with her hands.

Helping your baby's hand–eye coordination

There are a number of ways you can help.

- Let your baby reach for things, whether it is a book you are looking at together, or your nose or hair. Let her do this as much as possible, although you would be well advised to move hazardous or fragile objects out of her reach.

- Give positive feedback. Your approval is good for your baby.

- Encourage your baby's interest in new things. It may be something just outside her reach for now. Once she is attracted to it, she will make an all-out effort to grab it.

- Show her what various things can do. If she does not yet know what to do with a rattle, give her a demonstration.

- Your baby may enjoy a wrist toy or bell bracelet attached with Velcro. She will learn which hand movements produce the noise.

- Use finger play, for instance acting out a simple story with finger puppets.

- Even watching you do things is part of her learning process. First-hand experiments are best of all. However, research shows that a person's brain has so-called 'mirror neurones', which fire both when she makes a movement and when she watches watching someone else making the same movement. This may help to explain how babies learn by example.

Grasping

At 3 months, your baby cannot reach and grasp, but she soon tries. This is a vital development. You may notice that your baby sometimes makes passing swipes at things, but she usually misses. However, all these actions teach her something, so they are stepping stones on the way to acquiring more developed hand–eye skills.

From 3 months onwards, your baby's grasp is mostly involuntary, but she discovers that she can sometimes grab things that she wants. She uses her whole fist, or both hands for larger objects. Now she can clutch a rattle and perhaps keep it in her hand for a moment or two.

By 4 months, she can hold a rattle and shake it at the same time. If she likes the noise, or you show appreciation, it will not be long before she shakes it again.

By 5 months, your baby's grasp has improved further, so she uses her palm and outer three fingers. As she cannot use her forefinger and thumb yet, she cannot handle small objects.

Her grasp is still not entirely under her control. She drops toys accidentally. Even at 6 months, she will drop one object if you offer her another.

Reaching out

At 3 months, your baby wants to grab many things – a toy, her bottle, your hair. You may notice her intention in her eyes. Much of the time she will misjudge the distance and overshoot the object of her desire. But these misses serve a purpose, as every time she gets it wrong helps her do better next time.

By 5 months, her skills have improved, and many more of her attempts are now successful. She can reach for things on the table in front of her, or for toys dangling on a string nearby. Smartest of all, she can manoeuvre her trunk to get closer before she reaches out.

Senses

Your baby's visual horizons expand as his senses become more acute. As with hand–eye coordination, it is all about making connections. His brain is busy creating important links between nerve cells, so that, as the months pass, everything he sees, feels, hears, tastes or smells becomes more meaningful. Each new experience builds on what he has already learned, creating a nerve cell network that is uniquely his own.

Connections at every level

A baby's skills in different spheres of development become increasingly interdependent. For instance, his new ability to sit upright (see pages 60–61) has a bearing on his vision. If he did not see the world the right way up, his eyesight would not develop in the same way. Meanwhile, as he becomes better at grasping objects, he can fine-tune his senses by studying them at closer range.

Vision

From 3 months onwards, your baby focuses increasingly better on near objects. His eye muscles are more coordinated, so he rarely squints. However, his eyesight is still not yet perfect.

Until he is about 4 months old, very small items may not attract his attention. From then onwards, he becomes more perceptive. He can now follow with his eyes almost anything that catches his attention, through a range of 180 degrees, but he may lose track of it if it moves quickly.

More distant objects are more interesting to him now. At about 5 or 6 months, he gets excited if he sees you handle a favourite toy or unfold the buggy for an outing, as he now begins to understand what it means.

There are some things for which his eyesight is not yet ready. By 6 months, your baby still has little perception of depth or distance. His eyesight will not be as mature as an adult's until he is 2 years of age.

Hearing

Your baby is now acutely aware of sounds. From 3 months, you can expect him to turn and listen when you are speaking, because his head and upper body control is so much better. Even sounds that are further away now matter more to him. A distant noise, such as a dog barking outside, may catch his attention.

Your baby's hearing is acute, and he is better at locating sounds. However, even at 6 months he is less good at noticing sounds directly behind him. Unless parents realize this, they may believe that their baby is deaf.

Taste and smell

Your baby's senses of taste and smell develop rapidly, especially between 4 and 6 months of age, when you may be giving him his first solid foods. You will find that he loves some of your offerings, but is less keen on others.

If your baby uses a dummy, minimize its use so that he can enjoy different tastes as well as exploring with his mouth. There is no need to give him his dummy unless he is crying and you could also restrict its use to night.

Touch

By about 5 months, your baby may be touching everything within reach. He is finding out whether things are hot or cold, or hard or soft, and whether he wants to spend more time investigating them.

To study something better, he puts it in his mouth. This is only partly for taste. The main reason is that his lips and tongue are packed with huge numbers of sensory nerve endings, making them even more touch-sensitive than his fingertips.

Don't worry about this mouthing phase. It is entirely normal, even if it means that he slobbers on a lot of things. Make sure his playthings are reasonably clean and avoid leaving out anything that he might potentially choke on.

From 5 months onwards, your baby will probably put his toes in his mouth. He appears to love this – and no wonder. His mouth can feel his toes, and vice versa, so he gets double the amount of sensory delight. In doing so, he also builds up a mental map of his own body.

Learning

As your baby's perception of the world changes, her understanding of it deepens. She begins to put together her experiences. In this way, she learns about cause-and-effect and other fundamentals of physics.

The keen student

Your baby's interest in her surroundings increases. Put her in an unfamiliar room, and she literally sits up and takes notice. She sizes up people as well as places. From 3 months, she stares at strangers with rapt attention.

At 5 months, your baby drops her rattle and looks down to see where it went. She may reach out for it, even though it is too far for her. She has already learned that dropped toys only fall downwards, although she doesn't know that the reason is called gravity.

At about 6 months, she does not know yet about sound waves either, but she does know that banging a brick on the table makes a noise – and that it is fun to do.

Learning by association

From 3 or 4 months, your baby learns a great deal by repeating actions that she initially made by accident. If she leans against a ball on the floor, the ball rolls away. Soon, she does it again. Before long, she realizes that she herself made the ball roll. This kind of feedback is essential to her learning.

Next she will work out how hard to push the ball to make it go as far as the middle of the room. She learns that if she does something, then something else happens as a consequence of this. The if–then process is an important part of finding out how things work.

Feedback from you

No less important is the part you play. Your baby needs encouragement from you. It is all too easy to get caught up with the other demands of daily life, but at this stage what really matters is spending time with and encouraging your baby, and showing her that you love her and approve of what she does.

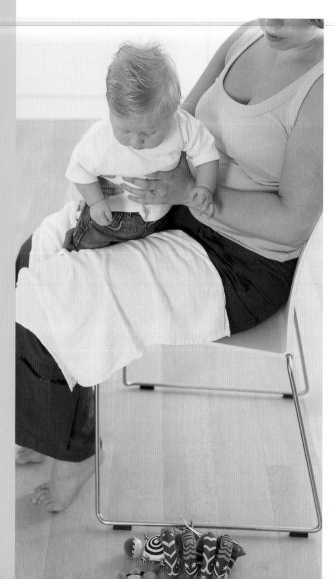

She needs to be allowed, within reasonable limits, to touch what she wants. The baby who is repeatedly told 'No' eventually becomes a child who has little thirst for knowledge or new experience and whose development may start to lag behind that of her peers.

This does not mean that any and all admonishments are out of the question. Boundaries are essential to all children, and you certainly don't want her experimenting with sharp objects, electrical sockets and other hazards.

Memory

At 3 months, your baby's memory has improved, but it is still very short term. She remembers things much better if she is allowed to use all her senses instead of one. This is why she can more easily recall a toy if she is allowed to grab it, suck it and chew it rather than just look at it.

If you take an object away, it's likely to be forgotten within a brief space of time. But gradually her memory improves. Let her have things that she can investigate safely to her heart's content.

Varying the pace

Although your baby is in a very responsive phase from about 3 months, her attention span is limited. She will not spend long doing one thing and quickly tires of a toy. Let her be your guide, and take your cue from her. Make sure there are times not just for playing and learning together, but also for quiet, undemanding cuddles – and for timely naps.

There will also be moments when your baby is happy to lie quietly and gaze at her surroundings. These peaceful contented interludes are good for her. They don't mean that she is waiting for you to produce a new toy or play yet another game.

Between 3 and 6 months, your baby is easy to distract. This makes it simple to move from one activity to the next. Her distractibility is also a bonus when you want her to stop doing something dangerous. However, a baby can easily get over-stimulated. When this happens, she may turn her head away or shut her eyes.

If given further stimulation, she may become crotchety or even cry. But, with a bit of experience, you will discover how to anticipate when she has had enough, so that you can wind things down and let her recharge her batteries. And you can recharge yours too.

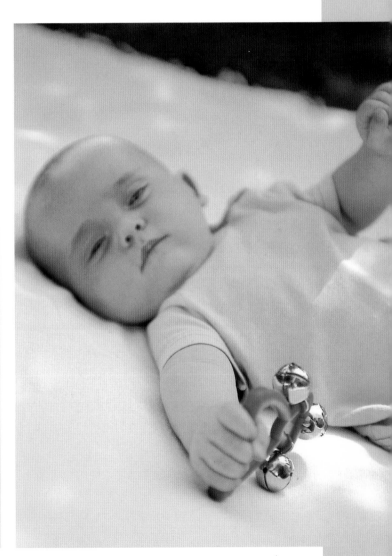

Toys

The best toys stimulate a baby's senses. A favourite toy might be something that moves or makes a noise, or has an interesting shape, colour and feel. It is not necessary to have complicated toys. Beakers that fit together are good, as are toys of different sizes, weights and textures. Try to rotate your baby's playthings. He will get fed up if all of them are out – and you will tire of the clutter!

Soft toys

Faces are a constant source of fascination to babies, so teddy bears, dolls and any other soft toys with faces are perennial favourites. These toys also help to teach your baby about caring and being sociable, gentle and kind.

Toys with a noise

Until about 6 months, your baby will enjoy rattles and wrist toys, such as a bracelet with small bells on it. He might also like squeaky toys. From about 4 months, he can probably squeeze the toy himself. Toys that right themselves when knocked over also appeal.

Playpens

Many parents say they could not cope without a playpen, while others cannot see the point of having them.

A playpen can be a good place for your baby to play safely. You can watch him while you cook or do other chores, and you can pop him into the playpen while you answer the door. A playpen will also keep a toddler and baby separated if necessary, and it can be a good place for your baby to take a nap during the day.

On the other hand, playpens limit a baby's exploration and learning, so they can be dull. After a while, the baby gets bored, even with toys beside him. If you decide to have a playpen, use it only for short periods of time. Otherwise, your baby could come to hate it.

Balls

A soft ball to roll on the floor is fun, especially if it also chimes or tinkles, or has a soft feel or an interesting texture. Before your baby learns how to move the ball himself, try rolling it slowly past him across his line of vision.

Baby gyms and activity centres

Now that your baby can reach out and actively explore with his hands, cradle gyms and activity centres become more interesting. There are also play–mats that incorporate different textures for your baby to enjoy. Some have toys attached to them.

Books

Three months is not too early to look at books with your baby, as long as they are short and simple, with bright uncomplicated pictures. Although you will be turning the pages, he will probably want to get in on the act, so board or cloth books are best at this stage. Bath books made of wipe–clean plastic are also good, whether you use them in the bath or on a mat on the floor.

Interacting with your child through play

These 3 months are an enchanting time to play with your baby, because he revels in being close to you but is also keen to explore new things.

■ Use finger puppets or glove puppets to act out a story or rhyme. A game of 'peek-a-boo' will make your baby laugh with glee, especially if you keep it simple and repeat it when he feels like it.

■ From about 4 months, toys such as a pop-up clown or jack-in-the-box appeal to your baby's sense of surprise and anticipation. He may be able to operate a jack-in-the-box if you help.

■ Use small squeaky toys as a game. You can hold one in each hand, press one of them, and get your baby to work out which of your hands is making the squeaks.

■ Nursery rhymes and bouncing songs help speech development as well as prompting plenty of laughter. Once your baby finds a favourite, you will see his eyes light up with anticipation.

■ There are many other simple games, such as building a tower of beakers or blocks and letting your baby knock it down. This also helps to teach him how the tower is made.

Communication

At 3 months, your baby embarks on a very sociable phase. She will reach out to strangers as well as people she knows and loves. Her communication skills are improving, and some of the noises she makes sound very like speech.

If you have twins

You will notice your twins interacting with each other from an early age. This is hardly surprising because they are just continuing what they started in the womb.

Twins sometimes experience a delay in learning to speak, so it is important to communicate with each of your babies. Try to spend some time with each twin separately.

When they are together, try to address each twin separately, making eye contact as often as possible. Use each baby's name often, so that she will know you are speaking to her.

Smiling

When your baby is happy, she smiles. Your voice and your face have special meaning for her, so you are likely to get the widest smiles. However, once she gets into the habit, she smiles at almost everyone. It is fun because people instantly smile back. And she will return the favour. Some time after 3 or 4 months, she will become more shy.

Pre-speaking skills

From 3 months, she is very responsive to conversation and can pick up a lot of meaning from your tone of voice. There is also evidence that young babies recognize words. Your baby will listen more intently to her native language than to a foreign one.

In conversation, your baby will vary the pitch and the tone of the sounds she makes.

By 6 months, she will start building her own repertoire of word sounds that are specific to your own language.

Babbling

Your baby continues to coo, but from 3 months she babbles. This mostly takes the form of vowel sounds and single syllables, and may consist of repeats of one syllable, such as 'ba-ba-ba'.

By 4 months, she may make a lot of two-syllable sounds, such as 'ah-goo'. She now enters a phase of vocal play, enjoying the sounds that she makes. Different sounds create different vibrations which she can sense.

At about 6 months, she adds a few more consonants, making more sounds such as 'ba', 'da', 'ga' and 'ka'.

Stimulating your baby's language development

A baby needs plenty of communication. Speak to her during daily activities, whether you are going to the park, driving to the child-minder or changing a nappy.

■ Baby talk is acceptable. Stretching out the vowel sounds helps her to identify new sounds. Repeated syllables, such as 'dishy-wishy' or 'doggy-woggy', emphasize sounds, again helping her to recognize them.

■ While speaking to your baby, minimize background noise, such as television and radio, so she can hear you properly.

■ Face her when you speak. Your expressions are a guide to what you mean. Backward-facing buggies are useful in this respect.

■ Whenever possible, make eye contact too. This maintains her attention and makes your words more meaningful.

■ Make conversation. She cannot answer questions yet, but ask them anyway, leaving a pause for a response. 'Did you have a nice nap?' helps her to learn about different kinds of sentences and patterns of speech. Before long, she will understand what you say.

■ Keep any use of dummies to a minimum, at least during waking hours.

■ Reply when your baby babbles. This encourages her to try out new sounds.

■ Use your baby's name. Research shows that babies are more attentive to sounds made just before or just after their name.

■ Read to her. Use your face and vary your tone to help her understand.

■ Play music and sing songs and nursery rhymes. These keep her interested in sounds and convey different meanings and moods.

Emotions

At 3 months, your baby is adept at showing how he feels. Enjoyment, frustration, contentment, discomfort or tiredness are written large on his increasingly expressive features. Already he shows his likes and dislikes. He finds comfort in routine and has built up a mental picture of the pattern of his days. By 5 months, he will expect a bath when he sees you reaching for the towels.

Relationship with you

Your baby is very attached to you. He has yet to think of himself as a separate person, so it is no surprise that, throughout these 3 months, he can read your moods and sense how you – and your partner – feel. You are all-important to him. From 4 months, he grabs at your sleeve when he wants your attention. He may also cry when you leave the room.

Relationships with other people

Emotional expressions are universal from culture to culture, and much the same at different ages. Your baby can therefore read people's moods by their expressions. While he is especially good at understanding your feelings, he can also interpret other people's faces.

At 3 months, he knows if a stranger is well-disposed towards him. He certainly studies strange faces closely, absorbing all he can. He likes the company of others, whether they are babies, children or adults. By 5 months, he may even cough to attract someone's attention.

By 6 months, he may begin to show shyness with people he does not know. This marks the start of a new phase in his emotional development.

Body language

Your baby uses his body as well as his face to convey emotions. By 4 months, he may bounce up and down to show he is excited. If he is delighted, he may breathe more quickly and kick out with his arms and legs. His eyes widen when he is really thrilled, as when he sees a favourite toy.

By 5 months, he may rock back and forth with amusement or pleasure. His reactions are often all or nothing. His moods change quickly, and there is no mistaking how he feels. He pushes you away when he is annoyed or tired, and he cries lustily when he wants something.

Sounds

An increasingly wider range of sounds accompanies his emotions. By 3 months, your baby can squeal with delight and coo with pleasure.

At about 4 months, he laughs out loud and chortles with anticipation. It is fun sharing his sense of humour. One thing that really pleases him is practising what he has learned, such as reaching out and grabbing things.

By 4 or 5 months, your baby is ticklish – and enjoys it. Before long, he laughs even before your approaching finger has touched the skin of his tummy.

Self-awareness

At 4 months, your baby notices his reflection in the mirror, but is not aware that he is looking at himself. He looks in the mirror as if it were any other plaything.

Child care

By 3 months, your baby may be attached to one, two or more people. Such attachments are normal and depend on how many adults are closely involved in his care.

If you are thinking of going back to work, you may be worried about someone new entering your baby's life. There are many different kinds of child care, and what you choose depends on your own situation.

Even so, however good your choice, your baby needs a few days to get used to someone else. The newness will seem less if he has his own toys and other familiar things. Being separated from you has its positive side. For one thing, your baby's sense of self will increase as he learns that he can enjoy himself without his parents being there all the time.

6–9 months
Sitting up and taking notice

Major milestones

- ✔ Teething begins
- ✔ Learns to sit up without support
- ✔ Uses thumb and index finger to grasp objects
- ✔ Learns that people and things are permanent
- ✔ Understands what you say
- ✔ Learns sounds specific to his own native language

Things to
look out for

From 6 to 9 months, your baby is still developing rapidly. Her movements become more controlled and coordinated, and her first teeth appear. In addition, as her mental associations improve, she begins to develop a distinct personality.

Physical changes

At 6–9 months old, your baby can sit upright and take in everything around her. Once she can manage to sit unsupported, she begins to spend a lot of time in this position, reaching out to get what she wants. By 9 months, she is also able to get herself into a sitting position without your help. Her movements are vigorous, although she is not yet fully mobile because control of her legs has yet to catch up with the development of her arms and trunk.

Her hands become increasingly skilful. At about 8 months, your baby can pick up things with her thumb and forefinger, enabling her to study a variety of small objects from every angle. There is so much to do and many new things to see. Your baby is more alert than ever, and her attention span is increasing too.

Several of her teeth appear during these 3 months, starting with one of the bottom front teeth. Some babies go through teething relatively easily, while others find the process more painful. As each tooth appears, your baby's smile changes slightly.

Your baby and her environment

As her brain connections multiply, the size of her brain increases and the activity in her brain cells also changes subtly. By 8 months, your baby can recognize many complex objects in the same way as an adult. Between the ages of 6 and 9 months, she also discovers the important principle known as 'object permanence': in other words, she understands that things continue to exist even when she cannot see them.

Her tastes in food expand as she moves on from milk feeds to more substantial meals. She can now drink from a cup or beaker, even if she often spills the contents. By 7 or 8 months, she may be enjoying a variety of finger foods, including biscuits, toast and chunks of vegetables or fruit. She will probably also put a spoon to her mouth, although very little of the food on it will reach its target!

There is now so much going on that it is no surprise to find that your baby sleeps somewhat less than before. At around 6 months, babies learn to stay awake when they want to, even if they are tired.

Communicating

Your baby's skills are becoming increasingly interrelated. She can now hear well, including more distant noises. She is also good at distinguishing speech sounds, which is important for her language development. Her increased visual awareness also helps her language skills. Now that her vision is so sharp, many objects catch her eye. She will often point at them, wanting to know more about them. This provides many chances for you to talk to her about what she sees.

In no time, your baby's language comes on apace. During these 3 months, she starts learning the sounds specific to your native tongue, so word-building begins in earnest. She babbles and tries out different sounds. She may not make any recognizable words, but she is experimenting all the time with sounds that will eventually create her first words. She is also varying her tone of voice and inflection. By 9 months, if not before, she will recognize and respond to her own name.

Behaviour

Your baby is now becoming more of a real person, with a personality to match. Now you will notice many differences between your baby and your friends' babies. Objects that hold no interest for other babies may fascinate yours. She may have different mannerisms too.

One thing is certain: your baby is very attached to you. This process begins in earnest at about the age of 6 months and continues until the age of 4 years. Its effects last throughout her entire life. From 6 months, your baby may show distress if you leave the room. She may also become clingy or shy when strangers are around. As ever, her body language speaks volumes about how she feels.

Summary of development

Growth and health

By 6 months
- Teething begins, altering the shape of his face.
- Can drink from a cup or beaker, with spills.

By 7 months
- Has four teeth.
- Enjoys increasingly wide range of foods, including finger foods.

By 8 months
- Has eight teeth.
- Can feed himself with his hands, albeit messily.

By 9 months
- Wants to put a spoon in his mouth.

Motor development

By 6 months
- Increasingly active and unhappy to stay for long in any one position.
- Becomes more robust, with stronger trunk muscles, while legs and lower body are less well developed.
- Can roll well from back to front and front to back.

By 7 months
- When lying flat on his front can heave himself forwards and sideways, using his arms, and begins to propel himself around the room.
- Sits upright unsupported.
- Has good forward control and can also play at the same time.

By 8 months
- May be creeping commando-style.

8–9 months
- Can get in and out of seated position unaided.

By 9 months
- Uses hands to stop himself toppling sideways.
- Can now do more while sitting up.
- May be crawling or perhaps bottom-shuffling.

Hand–eye coordination

By 6 months
- Plays with fingers and toes.
- Grasp is still basic, using whole hand to grip.

From 6 months
- Can see things that are further away.

6–7 months
- Can transfer objects from one hand to the other.

8–9 months
- Uses thumb and index finger as a pincer for small objects.
- Uses index finger to point to or poke at things.

By 9 months
- Begins to drop objects deliberately.
- Has some appreciation of depth and distance, but his vision is not as good as an adult's.
- Studies very small objects closely, using his improved hand–eye skills in order to investigate detail.
- Points to things that hold interest for him.

Senses and learning

By 6 months
- Can hear sounds that are further away.
- Is ever more alert, interested in everything and fascinated by faces.
- Attention span is increasing.

By 7 months
- Looks around briefly for a dropped object.

By 8 or 9 months
- Can localize sounds well if behind or next to him, but less good at localizing sounds immediately above or below him.
- Has learned about 'object permanence'.

Communication

By 6 months
- Babbles fluently and sings, both with great expression.
- Starts to learn sounds that are specific to his native language.
- Says 'ma', 'da', 'ka', 'der'.

From 6 months
- Understanding is very good.

By 7 months
- Puts sounds together into two syllables.

By about 8 months
- Proper word-learning starts.

Until at least 9 months
- Body language still remains the principle means of communication.
- Uses his whole body and points persistently to indicate what he wants.

By 9 months
- May make sounds that resemble real words.
- Starts to respond to his own name.

Emotions

By 6 months
- Enjoys attention and company.
- Likes routine and dislikes change.
- Shows pleasure and displeasure with a mix of body language and sounds.

From 6 months
- May become anxious when separated from you.
- Anxious or shy with strangers and may cling to you.
- Real personality emerging.

6–7 months
- Interested in adults, children and other babies.

7–8 months
- Can play happily on his own for more of the time.

By 9 months
- Growing sense of self, although he does not yet recognize himself in a mirror.

Growth and health

The most obvious changes in your baby's appearance in these 3 months are found in her face. These noticeable changes are caused by the appearance of her milk teeth.

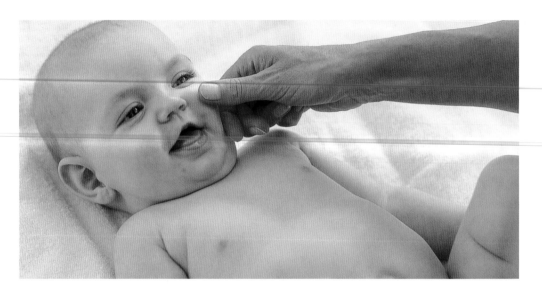

Onset of teething

From 6 months, the milk teeth start breaking through the gums. For a few days, or even weeks, beforehand, your baby may dribble a lot and chew everything that comes to hand, including her fist. A baby's teeth are fully formed before they appear. Together with the bone, her jaw is literally full of teeth. You can see the outline of a tooth beneath the gum surface shortly before it erupts.

The first tooth to come through is one of the lower middle incisors, followed swiftly by its neighbour. From about 6½ months, the upper central incisors appear one after the other. Your baby now has four teeth – but not for long. At 7 months, the lower lateral incisors appear, next to her first teeth. The upper lateral incisors follow about a month later. By 8 months, your baby may have eight teeth.

Teeth – order of appearance

6 MONTHS: lower central incisors
6½ MONTHS: upper central incisors
7 MONTHS: lower lateral incisors
8 MONTHS: upper lateral incisors
10 MONTHS: lower anterior molars
14 MONTHS: upper anterior molars
16 MONTHS: lower canines
18 MONTHS: upper canines
24 MONTHS: lower second molars
30 MONTHS: upper second molars

These dates are averages. About one in every 2,000 babies is born with at least one tooth. On the other hand, babies may be 12 months old or more when their first tooth comes through. Even so, your baby should have all 20 milk teeth by the time she is 2½ years old.

Teething troubles

Babies differ in their response to teething. Some find it a painful process, while others breeze through it. Common symptoms of teething include:

• Dribbling.
• A red cheek.
• Pain and irritability.
• Crying more than usual.

A teething ring cooled in the fridge can ease discomfort. There are also many over-the-counter teething gels and powders, including homoeopathic remedies, available from pharmacies. Liquid paracetamol also helps teething babies.

It is debatable whether teething causes loose motions or nappy rash. What is certain is that teething will not make your baby run a high fever, develop a cough, have a fit (convulsion) or produce any other serious symptoms. If this happens, check with your doctor, because it is not due to teething.

Milk teeth matter

A child starts losing her milk teeth when she is about 6 years old but, even so, milk teeth are important. They help the jaw change shape, which is an essential development as far as eating and speaking are concerned. Milk teeth also serve as guides for the permanent teeth, which is why it is vital to care for your baby's teeth as soon as they appear.

Tooth-brushing

Using a baby toothbrush, start cleaning your baby's teeth morning and evening as soon as they appear. At first, you can hold her on your lap and brush from behind. When she is old enough to stand unaided, brush them from the front. Let her brush her own teeth when she seems ready, but continue to supervise her until you are confident that she is brushing properly and can do so on her own.

Your baby's measurements

At 6 months
AVERAGE WEIGHT: 7.3 kg (16 lb)
LENGTH: about 65 cm (26 in) long
HEAD CIRCUMFERENCE: about 43 cm (17 in)

At 9 months
AVERAGE WEIGHT: 8.7 kg (19 lb)
LENGTH: about 70 cm (27½ in)
HEAD CIRCUMFERENCE: about 45 cm (17½ in)

These figures are just a guide. Healthy babies come in a range of sizes and weights.

Tips for healthy teeth

It is never too early to start practising good dental hygiene.

■ Ensure that your baby's diet is rich in calcium, vitamins and minerals.

■ Your baby may need fluoride drops, depending on where you live. Ask your dentist, health visitor or doctor.

■ As soon as your baby can handle a cup or trainer beaker, use these for all her drinks.

Care – feeding and weaning

Starting solid foods is an important step for your baby. By 6 months, almost all babies need more nourishment than they can obtain from breast milk or formula. Your baby is also now developmentally ready to try new things. This is why it is best not to leave weaning later than 6 months, unless your doctor advises it.

Chewing and swallowing

As with other aspects of development, there is a window of opportunity. Your baby has to learn how to chew and swallow solids, which is an entirely different process from drinking milk. He also has to get used to the taste and texture of solids. If a baby stays on milk-only feeds beyond 8 months or so, he may never take well to solid meals.

Note that the actions of chewing and swallowing develop the jaw muscles, which are vital in learning to speak.

First foods

A good first food is baby rice. Avoid giving wheat products or anything containing gluten until your baby is at least 6 months old, because of the risk of gluten sensitivity (coeliac disease).

To begin with, feed your baby using a small spoon, during or after his milk feed. Touch a spoon containing a small amount of food to his lower lip. He will open his mouth, although it may be a few days before he laps up the contents of the spoon.

After 3–4 weeks, you can add puréed fruit or vegetables to another meal of the day. Single ingredients are best at this stage. The taste should still be bland, so don't add sugar or salt. If your baby does not like something, leave it for a few days and try again.

By about 6–8 weeks after starting solids, your baby can try more complex mixtures, as well as foods with a slightly coarser texture. Before long your baby will be enjoying many different combinations. You can include gluten products once your baby is 6 months old.

About 2–3 months after starting solids, your baby can enjoy meat, poultry, fish, baby yoghurt, rusks, pasta and semolina. By now you can mash his food instead of sieving it.

Feeding himself

By about 8 months, your baby wants to feed himself. Finger foods, such as rusks, toast and pieces of cucumber, are ideal, but you must supervise him in case he chokes.

By 9 months, your baby wants to hold the spoon himself, but he cannot handle it properly. He dips it into his food but rotates it just before it reaches his lips, so that its contents slide off. A good plan is to let him hold one spoon – which he can wave about, put in his ear or bang on the table – while you use another for feeding him.

Dealing with the mess

This stage is not a tidy one. Take it in your stride and be prepared for the mess. A bib with a trough is good at catching the inevitable spills. Some parents put a plastic sheet under the high-chair too. Newspaper is probably better because it can be thrown away afterwards rather than sponged down.

Vitamins

In some countries, supplements of vitamins A, C and D are actively recommended for your baby.

Drinks

Solids will not make up an appreciable proportion of your baby's feeds until he is having about three solid meals a day. Milk continues to be a major part of his intake until he is about 9 months old. Although he can have products such as yoghurt and cheese made from cows' milk, he should not have cows' milk as his main drink because it contains too much protein and not enough iron for his needs.

By 6 months, your baby can drink either from a cup or a beaker. If you have used bottles until now, this is a good time to switch to a cup for all his drinks, except breast milk.

Healthy baby drinks

To prevent your baby getting used to sweet things, don't give him a lot of sugary drinks.

- Limit fruit juices (and sweet foods) to mealtimes. This is when the flow of saliva is greatest, so it dilutes the sugars.

- Avoid fizzy drinks and diet drinks at any age. These are acidic, so they both can damage enamel even though they do not contain any added sugar.

- Long lingering drinks are the most damaging to teeth, so never leave a bottle of milk or juice in your baby's cot.

- By the time your baby is 9 months old, he may need only water as a night-time drink, when he needs one at all.

Motor development

Your baby's months of experimenting with her body now take her development another step forward. As her balance improves and her body becomes stronger, she spends less time on her back. In fact, she rarely stays long in any one position, preferring to be active and to try out new postures.

Rolling

At 6 months, your baby moves as much as possible during her waking hours. Soon she can roll well from back to front, and from front to back, assisted by her hands.

By 7 months, if not before, she may roll her way around the room.

Getting around

By 7 months, she discovers that, when lying on her front, she can heave herself forwards and sideways using her hands. Pushing backwards enables her to reverse. These days she might spend more time off her play-mat than on it. Look away for a moment and you may find she has travelled quite a distance!

By 8 months, she could be creeping on her belly, commando-fashion, an inelegant but effective way to get around. Her arms and trunk are stronger than her legs, which lag behind in their development, but towards 9 months she starts to make more use of them. Keeping it all coordinated is quite a challenge for your baby, and her first attempts at crawling may well take place in reverse gear.

By 9 months, some babies are crawling forwards. Others begin to shuffle about on their bottoms. These variations are both completely normal. Your baby's choice of style now has no bearing on how well she will walk later.

Encouraging safe movement

You should encourage your baby to move about safely as much as possible.

☐ If you have a playpen, do not put your baby in it for too long. Only put your baby in a car seat, high-chair or buggy when necessary.

☐ Let your baby play on her front to strengthen her shoulder, thigh and back muscles. When she wants to change position, rather than moving her, guide her body by giving her gentle support so that she makes most of the movement herself.

☐ Play bouncy games that help her make the most of her strength and energy.

☐ Move any flimsy pieces of furniture, such as card tables or small pedestal tables, before she tries to use them as a support. Dangling tablecloths are another hazard.

Standing

By 7 or 8 months, your baby may bounce on her feet momentarily if you hold her up securely by her chest, but her legs rarely take all her weight. She is not ready to do more at this stage, so don't force it. From about 8 months, she may pull herself up to a standing position, using you or a piece of furniture as a support. She also stands up in her cot by holding onto the bars.

Progressing to sitting

At 6 months, your baby sits supported for a few minutes. If she is put into a high-chair, she may loll to one side. However, she has good forward control, so rarely falls in this direction. She looks forward to sitting up and holds out her hands for you to help her get into a seated position. If surrounded by cushions, she enjoys sitting on the floor.

By 7 months or so, your baby can sit unsupported for increasing periods of time. She may be able to play with a toy on the floor in front of her at the same time.

By about 8 months, she can sit unsupported for up to 10 minutes. Thanks to her newly acquired balance, she may rock back and forth without toppling. When she has become accomplished at rolling and sitting, she can combine the two movements.

By 8 or 9 months, she can get in and out of a sitting position unaided.

At 9 months, she is good at using her hands as props to stop herself falling sideways. Now she is stable in a wide range of seated positions, so she can play happily while sitting. Moreover, she often moves forwards, or even twists sideways, for a toy that grabs her attention. If it is out of reach, she rolls onto the floor to get it.

Hand–eye coordination

Between 6 and 9 months, your baby's coordination becomes more fine-tuned. He not only has better control of his trunk but is also making full use of his hands in an increasingly adult way. As a result, he usually gets whatever he is going after.

Grasping and letting go

At 6 months, your baby's grasp is still basic, and he hardly uses his thumb. Instead, he uses his whole hand as a scoop, grabbing objects with his palm and his fingers. His hands are strong, and his grasp, although crude, is quite effective. He manages to pick up toys of various sizes, shapes and weights. Depending on the size of the object, he may home in on it with one or both hands.

From around 7 months, he can hold an object in one hand without dropping it if you offer him a second object. Moreover, he

can also transfer something from one hand to the other.

From around 8 months, your baby starts to use his thumb, a skill which humans share with apes. Together with his forefinger, he grasps small objects in a pincer action.

By 9 months, his pincer grip is good and usually accurate. During meals, he may, for instance, pick up a pea or a raisin from his bowl and examine it in great detail from several angles. Whether or not he eats it when he has finished studying it is another matter!

From 8 or 9 months onwards, your baby uses his forefinger to prod an object before picking it up. If he cannot reach it, he points at it, insistently if need be, for you to respond to the hint.

From about 9 months, he uses his hands to evaluate objects. If your baby is presented with two similar items, such as building blocks, he may pick one up in each hand and hold them side by side, as if he is comparing them.

At 8 months, he is not yet good at letting go when he wants to. When he drops something, it is partly involuntary. Releasing his grasp seems to occur as something of an afterthought.

At 9 months, he learns to let go, a skill that he will soon be practising for all he is worth.

Adapting to the task

At 6 months, your baby is refining his hand control. He can modify the effort he makes to suit the purpose. He can, for instance, gently manipulate small things, such as the beads on an abacus. But he can also bang down a toy hard on the floor when he wants to.

Using his improved hand–eye skills, he continues his investigations into the material world. At 8 or 9 months, he lobs a toy a short distance, as if to see how far it will go. Usually, he then fetches it back.

Using the rest of his body

Your baby's coordination depends a lot on what he has learned from his own body. Until 8 or 9 months, he still plays with his fingers and toes, especially when lying on his back.

At 6 months, he still puts things in his mouth. His favourite toys may get very damp, as he is likely to be dribbling much of the time. However, as his manual dexterity improves, this mouthing activity tails off. By 9 months, he will not put as much in his mouth as he did at 4 or 5 months.

Safety

Now that your baby is ever more mobile, as well as intrigued by everything, safety becomes a major consideration. It is wise to think ahead.

- ☐ Use a high-chair harness.

- ☐ Cover sharp corners on low tables.

- ☐ Cover electrical sockets.

- ☐ Move any breakable items, such as vases, that could injure him.

- ☐ Install stair gates to barricade stairs – and perhaps the kitchen.

- ☐ Hide away knives and other sharp items.

- ☐ Keep cups of hot drink well out of reach.

- ☐ Fit guards on real or electric fires.

- ☐ Turn down radiator thermostats.

Senses and learning

There are several reasons why your baby learns a lot in these 3 months. Her senses continue to develop, enabling her to make discoveries about the world around her. Her brain is now growing rapidly, and from about 7 months onwards fundamental changes occur in her brain, helping her to organize information and recognize complex things in much the same way as adults.

Vision

Your baby notices everything in the room up to about 3 m (10 ft), and she looks around her with huge interest. From 6 months, your baby adjusts her position to see things better. By 8 months, she cranes her neck and twists her body to see the many things that intrigue her. Comings and goings interest her greatly. She also follows a moving toy, although she cannot keep pace with anything that moves too rapidly through her field of vision.

She has little appreciation of depth or distance, but this changes rapidly. By 9 months, your baby has better depth perception. However, you must to continue to protect her because she still cannot finally appreciate depth and has no fear of falling, whether from her high chair, a cliff or the edge of the sofa.

Hearing

At 6 months, your baby can register sounds that are further away. By 8 or 9 months, her hearing is well developed. She is good at discriminating and localizing sounds, but her hearing is still not fully mature, and she is not good at localizing sounds that are directly below or above her. She may take no notice if you speak to her from above when she is in her buggy. If this happens, catch her attention visually first.

Taste and smell

Your baby's senses of taste and smell are developing throughout this time. She continues to taste and smell toys. If she is teething, she may also gnaw on whatever is handy to relieve minor discomfort. By 9 months she begins to put fewer things in her mouth.

The new sensations are mainly from the foods that you offer her. By 7 months, she seems to savour the eating experience, licking her lips. She may open her mouth wide in anticipation of another spoonful of a food that she enjoys.

At 8 months, she may linger over finger foods. Her sense of smell enables her to look forward to a favourite meal that you have prepared for her. She has strong likes and dislikes, but these do not tend to last.

Touch

Touch remains a vital sense for your developing baby. At 6 months, her incredibly sensitive fingers explore everything. When she begins to use her thumbs, by about 8 months, she can do even more. She touches every surface of every object and also puts things to her mouth, if not actually inside it, to complete the experience.

By about 8 months, when your baby can creep and is truly on the move, there is no stopping her discoveries. Everything around her is worthy of analysis: from the toy in front of her to an older sibling's building

blocks, your keys, the rough texture of the carpet or the velvety fell of the curtains at the other end of the room.

Putting it all together

Your baby's learning becomes increasingly a matter of combining her senses and skills, and she uses her newly acquired hand–eye coordination to great effect. She not only picks up and looks at new things, she also smells and tastes them.

By 8 months, her attention span is so good that she devotes a long time to studying one thing. She can also play for longer periods of time on her own, usually very happily.

She may pull at an object to investigate its strength. She may also shake it or drop it to find out if it makes a noise. Sometimes she will bang it on the floor, or a window or glass table, to test its hardness. All this is important for your baby's learning, but there are safety implications.

Learning and toys

Now that your baby is sitting up and taking notice of things, almost everything interests him. Importantly, his attention span and memory are increasing, so his understanding deepens, and he remembers what he learns.

Object permanence

Between 6 and 9 months, your baby learns something fundamental: things continue to exist, even when he cannot see them. This principle is called 'object permanence'. This may be obvious, but it is an important stage in your baby's intellectual maturity, as well as an indication of his memory skills.

You can see its gradual emergence. At 6 months, your baby looks at the floor to see the direction in which a dropped toy has gone. At 7 months, he makes a cursory visual search for the toy. At about 8 months, he looks for it more thoroughly, even if he cannot find it.

By 9 months, your baby may be able to locate a toy that you showed him before covering it with a blanket. Once he starts doing this, you will be able to play games with hidden objects. However, don't make them too hard because they will only frustrate him.

Memory

By 9 months, your baby remembers a hidden object, as well as his favourite toys. This suggests that his memory is evolving. He also has a good memory for routine, for instance, that bathtime is followed by a drink, then a story, then bed.

Remembering is vital to all areas of learning, including speech. At 9 months, your baby will recognize and remember most common household objects. By remembering what became of something the last time he played with it, your baby will know what to expect the next time. In this way, he builds on his previous experience.

However, memory does not develop all at once. It is important for parents to realize this, especially when it comes to safety. You can tell your baby not to do something, but he will not remember for long. In no time, he could again be touching something dangerous, such as an electrical appliance. This is not naughtiness. He simply cannot remember your warning. It is up to you to make his world safe without making it uniformly dull.

Choosing toys

Now that your baby is so active and aware, he will enjoy many different toys. He may also still love some of his earlier toys, such as rattles or soft toys.

Construction toys

Toys that fit into each other, such as beakers, will stimulate his senses and develop his powers of deduction.

Moving toys

A simple soft ball, with or without a chime, is fun to roll. Your baby may also like pushing wheeled toys, such as simple cars and trucks. Make sure beforehand that they are safe, and suitable for your baby's age. Many small model cars have tiny parts that can be a choking hazard, making them unsuitable for young babies.

Toys with a noise

Try introducing your baby to noisy things, such as squeaky toys and simple musical instruments. Your baby will want to spend a lot of time sitting, and this is perfect for playing with a tambourine, drum, xylophone or baby piano.

Books

Books are good, especially if you read to him while he looks at bold, bright pictures. Board or fabric books are sturdy enough for him to handle himself, while other books may need to be kept out of reach when you are not with to him.

Improvised toys

For a change, improvise toys from empty cereal packets and yoghurt pots. Babies also enjoy small pots and pans, or their lids. Large sheets of crumpled paper appeal to babies, which is why the wrapping paper can be as fascinating as the gift inside it. Bigger playthings are also good, such as a play tunnel or even just a large cardboard box open at each end for him to crawl in and out of.

From about 6 months, most babies enjoy splashing at bathtime. Provide some bath toys for him, and let him have fun with them too.

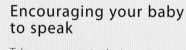

Communication

Your baby is making noticeable advances in both her understanding and her use of language. Even before she uses real words, you and she can have long, meaningful exchanges.

Understanding

By about 6 months, your baby's understanding is amazing. She responds to you with a range of sounds. The tone and rhythm of your speech are clues, and she recognizes words.

At about 9 months, she responds to her own name. She recognizes common objects, and knows up to 15 or 20 of them by name because she remembers you saying them.

Pre-speaking skills

Learning language is a two-fold process: understanding others and producing speech. Your baby understands you long before she makes any real words. While learning to speak, your baby uses a lot of body language. This helps in the process of speech. The same thing happens when adults study a new language.

Babbling and expression

Even young babies are acutely attuned to the pitch, tone and rhythm of the human voice. At 6 months, your baby engages in vocal play, babbling fluently with great intonation but no proper words. She also chuckles, coos and sings, again with huge expression. She enjoys the sound of her voice – and so will you.

Encouraging your baby to speak

Take every opportunity to encourage your baby's speaking abilities.

- Provide a loving and stimulating environment. Your baby does not need constant stimulation, but she does need speech and feedback from you.

- When speaking to your baby, make eye contact. Allow pauses for her to respond.

- Your baby will point to things that interest her, wanting to know more. This is your ideal opportunity to name things and increase her vocabulary. Developmental psychologists sometimes call this pointing 'referential looking'.

- If your baby is late in making words, it is worth checking her hearing, so talk to your health visitor or family doctor.

Language and how babies learn it

One definition describes language as a set of symbols for conveying thought. So language is not just speech. In the sense used by linguists, language also includes reading and writing. Obviously, since babies speak before they read, speech is the earliest sign of your baby's language skills. Experts still debate exactly how a child learns language, but it is likely to be a combination of several factors:

☐ Innate human ability to speak.

☐ The child's intelligence and her understanding of the world about her.

☐ Imitation of others.

Word sounds

At first, a baby's sounds belong to no particular language. All babies are born with the capacity to learn any tongue, but they soon become more focused. Language is learned largely by imitation. What a baby hears or does not hear profoundly affects the sounds she makes. A baby from, say, an Arabic-speaking family learns different sounds from an English-speaking household. Specific word sounds are sometimes known as 'phonemes'.

From 6 months, a baby starts learning the sounds specific to her native tongue. By about 8 months, a deaf baby may make sounds that are recogibsably different from those of other babies.

At 6 months, your baby makes mostly one-syllable sounds.

By 7 months, she starts making two-syllable sounds, putting together the sounds she has learned.

Proper word-learning begins at about 8 months. You are unlikely to hear any actual words before 8 months, although your baby may accidentally make sounds like 'mum-ma' or 'da-da'.

From about 9 months, your baby makes sounds in a meaningful way. Now when she says 'mum-ma', it is often when you are there. You can consider these to be her first proper words.

Bilingual families

Some babies are brought up in a home where two or more languages are spoken. Some parents, and even health professionals, believe that this causes difficulties for babies. In fact, early childhood, when the brain is malleable, is the best time to learn any language.

There is no evidence to show that babies get confused when exposed to more than one language, or that it delays them learning to speak. Bilingual children speak as fluently as other children. If you are bringing up your baby to speak more than one language, and she is not saying much, then look for another reason, such as hearing problems.

Emotions

Now that your baby communicates so eloquently with both his voice and his body language, his emotions are easy to read. His likes and dislikes are clearer than ever, and by 9 months you will find his personality comes through strongly.

Relationship with you

Your relationship with your baby began very early, even before birth. However, from about 6 months something more develops – your baby shows signs of real attachment to you.

According to attachment theory, the formation of attachment usually occurs between 6 months and 4 years of age. The person to whom a baby is attached is usually his mother, but it may also be the baby's father, a grandparent or an unrelated carer – anyone who has a lot to do with the baby (see below). This may surprise some parents, but the way you feed your baby, or even who feeds your baby, seems to have no bearing on attachment.

Relationships with other people

Many babies become attached to several people, often the mother first, then the father, and perhaps at a later date the grandparents or child-minder. There is good evidence that becoming attached to some other carer, such as a baby-minder, does nothing to weaken a baby's relationship with his mother. This should reassure working mothers. Find someone caring, who stimulates your baby as well as looks after his physical needs.

By 6 or 7 months, your baby is very interested in other people and what they do. He is curious about adults, and he relishes the company of other children. Even though it will be another 2 years or so before he makes friends outside the family, he likes playing near babies of about his age.

From 6 months onwards, your baby learns about 'person permanence' just as he learned about object permanence (see page 90). At about 7 months, he knows that someone exists, even when that person is no longer in the same room. By 8 months, he has built up a good mental picture of the people who figure in his life. This is important in terms of his attachments to you and any others who care for him. It is also vital to his developing sense of self as an independent human being.

Likes and dislikes

At 6 months, your baby enjoys routine. He remembers the daily pattern of rituals, such a bathtime, and looks forward to them, showing this with a mix of sounds and body movements, such as rocking back and forth, bouncing up and down, craning his neck or laughing. This is a very rewarding time for you as long as your baby is excited or happy, but it is less easy when he is feeling negative. He dislikes change and may be tearful if his routine is altered, if he feels insecure or unsettled, or if he is being rushed.

Fear of separation

From the age of 7 months or so, your baby may show signs of separation anxiety. He may cry when you leave the room, or he may call for you or try to follow you. These are all because he is attached to you. Other signs include snuggling up against you, hugging you and climbing onto your lap. Your baby can become clingy, especially when he is tired or ill, or his routine is disturbed. You (or others) may also notice that your baby plays more happily when you are nearby, a more subtle sign of separation anxiety.

Fear of strangers

From about 6 or 7 months, your baby may become shy or even apprehensive with people he does not know. He may cling to you tightly or just become quiet in the presence of strangers. This is completely normal and is not a symptom of any untoward shyness, as some parents fear. In fact, it is a sign of a healthy attachment to one or more important people. Unfortunately, it can come at a time when many mothers are returning to work, which can make leaving a baby difficult initially. Be patient at this stage. You may want to start leaving your baby for just a few hours at a time to begin with, rather than whole days. Given time, and the right child-minder, stranger anxiety need not pose a problem.

9–12 months

On the move

Major milestones
- ✔ Chews a range of food
- ✔ Can stay awake on purpose
- ✔ Can stand from a sitting position
- ✔ Walks using furniture ('cruising')
- ✔ Explores with his hands
- ✔ Drops things on purpose
- ✔ Makes more meaningful sounds and may start to say first words

Things to look out for

From 9 to 12 months, there are major changes in your baby's appearance. She also displays an increasing curiosity in her surroundings, increasing independence and much better communication skills. By 12 months, you will find that she is turning from a baby into an active toddler.

Physical changes

During these 3 months, your baby's physical appearance changes a great deal, transforming her shape. Her body now looks longer and sleeker as she holds herself more upright. She also has several teeth, which alters the shape of her mouth and face.

She probably also has a lot of hair. It may be baby-fine, but it is growing strongly. She may need her first haircut around now.

Your baby and her environment

Your baby is now really going places. She may not be walking on her own by her first birthday, but she will be able to get around long before then by crawling, rolling, furniture-cruising, walking on all fours or bottom-shuffling. One way or another, she will explore everything around her to the full in order to satisfy her curiosity.

It is fascinating to witness your baby's thirst for knowledge. Together with her newly found mobility, her hand–eye skills turn her into a mini-scientist as well as an intrepid explorer.

She may become less cuddly about now. This is normal and not something you should take personally. Her deep attachment to you means that she feels secure enough to use you as a base for her activities.

She wants to know what objects are for and what they can do. She is now getting her hands into everything. Rather than using her mouth to test out new objects, she uses her hands as increasingly sophisticated instruments to prod, poke and pull things apart. She may drop them to see what happens – an important lesson in cause and effect. Once she realizes that you will pick things up, she may begin to drop them on purpose, delighting in your efforts at retrieving them.

She is still clumsy, so you may want to move fragile objects out of her reach. At 9 months, your baby has no sense of danger. For a parent, this can be a challenging time because you have to think ahead to keep your baby safe.

Your baby wants to do more and more for herself. Although she wants to feed herself, she cannot quite execute the task of bringing a fully laden spoon to her lips without messy mishaps. She may protest when you take the spoon from her, so this is a time for tact on your part.

Perhaps surprisingly in view of all this activity, your baby's need for daytime sleep may actually fall. By 12 months, many babies are down to one daytime nap instead of two, so extra vigilance is required on the safety front during these active hours.

Communicating

There are many undeniable delights during these 3 months. From 9 months, your baby shows a keen sense of fun and an emerging sense of humour, so there is a lot of laughter. Your baby's concentration and memory are both far better than before, so she will really enjoy listening to stories and playing simple games with you. Thanks to her increasing understanding of the world, she can now also begin to play 'pretend' with such things as a toy telephone or a tea-set.

Your baby's language skills are also improving. She now understands many words, simple statements and even questions. From 9 months, she can comprehend 'Where is …?', enabling you to play hiding games together.

Your baby continues to babble. At this time, you can expect her first few words. Her pronunciation may be far from perfect, but you will still be thrilled. Before long, her words will no longer come one at a time. By 12 months, some babies can make simple two-word sentences. Nevertheless, your baby still relies a lot on body language. She may grunt when she offers you a toy or point to a toy that she wants. When someone leaves the room, she may wave goodbye. When someone she likes returns, her excited movements show just how pleased she is.

Summary of development

Growth and health

By 9 months
- Head has changed shape.
- Hair continues to grow, making him look more like a toddler.
- Has eight teeth on average.

From 9 months
- Can chew a wide variety of foods, increasing jaw development.
- Body is straighter and less rounded.

By 10 months
- First back teeth (lower anterior molars) start to appear.

Care

By 9 months
- Sleep pattern has changed and he can stay awake when he wants to.

- Controls body far better and becomes very active.
- May be crawling or bottom-shuffling.

10–12 months
- Abandons one daytime nap.

Motor development

By 9 months
- When sitting, can lean over sideways without toppling.
- When sitting, can easily pivot to reach a toy.

9–10 months
- Can pull himself up to standing in his cot, or on the floor, using furniture.
- Has trouble sitting down again unaided.

From 10 months
- Can move from lying down to standing or sitting.

10–11 months
- Can walk sideways while holding onto furniture.

By 11 months
- Can sit down from a standing position with less of a thud.
- May begin to walk if both hands are held.

By 12 months
- May be able to walk unaided.

Hand–eye coordination

By 9 months
- Has good pincer-action grasp, so can pick up small objects.
- Cannot always release objects without adult help.

By 10 months
- Will put an object into his parent's hand, but may not let it go.
- Puts toys in and out of containers.

- Can now release things when he wants to (but may tease his parent).

From 10 months
- Drops things deliberately for his parent to pick up.

Senses and learning

By 9 months
- Knows about object permanence.

From 9 months
- Concentration is better.
- Spends long periods of time exploring objects.
- Interested in things and events both near and far.
- Uses mouth less and hands more when investigating objects.

9–10 months
- Understands what many objects are for and begins to understand concepts and groups of things.
- Expresses interest in pictures in books.

From 10 months
- Copies parent and engages in pretend play.
- Increasingly wants to do things himself.
- Cooperates with dressing by holding out foot or arm.
- Copies parent and engages in pretend play.

By 12 months
- Memory improved.
- Recognizes most household objects and knows what they are for.
- Mouthing has almost stopped.
- Pokes, prods and pulls objects, taking time to find out about each one.
- Drops things, learning about gravity as well as cause-and-effect.

Communication

By 9 months
- Understanding is good.
- Knows about 15 household objects by name.
- Responds to own name.
- Understands simple questions.

From 9 months
- Continues to babble, using a mix of one- and two-syllable sounds.
- Makes sounds in an increasingly purposeful way.

9–10 months
- May say first word.

By 10 months
- May obey simple requests ('Sit down', 'Stand up', 'Give to me').

By about 11 months
- Learns to kiss when asked.

By 12 months
- Uses an average of three words with meaning.

Emotions

By 9 months
- Loves having tummy tickled.
- Has well-developed sense of person permanence. Is securely attached to one or more adults.

From 9 months
- Less overtly affectionate than before, but uses his parent as a base from which to explore.
- Continues to use body language to express emotion, especially by head shaking, turning head away, rocking or kicking.

- Amused at playing peek-a-boo.
- Personality develops and learns to assert his will.
- Usually happy in disposition, but can be volatile at times.

By 11 months
- Shows great sense of humour.

By 12 months
- Still shy with strangers.

Growth and health

During these 3 months, your baby's growth continues to be rapid, and her body shape and proportions are changing. Now that she is more upright, she appears less rounded. Her head seems less large compared with her body, and she is beginning to look more like a toddler.

Head and jaw

A young baby's head seems so big because the dome of her skull is so large. However, all that is changing and her skull bones will soon fuse together. By 12 months, the posterior fontanelle (the soft spot at the back of the head) closes. The anterior fontanelle (the soft spot at the front) takes longer and you may still be able to feel it until 18 months.

At the same time, your baby's jaw area becomes more prominent, even more so now that she has teeth. By 9 months, your baby has an average of eight teeth, four on the top jaw and four on the bottom. At about 10 months, the first back teeth (the anterior molars) start appearing in the lower jaw. Chewing helps your baby to develop good jaw muscles, further changing her facial appearance.

Hair

Now that your baby spends only a little time on her back, there are no thin or bare patches on the back of her head. You can clearly see the whorls of healthy hair growth.

Your baby's hair may now look quite thick, and very different from the baby-fine

Your baby's measurements

At 9 months
AVERAGE WEIGHT: 8.7 kg (19 lb)
LENGTH: about 70 cm (27½ in)
HEAD CIRCUMFERENCE: about 45 cm (17½ in).

At 12 months
AVERAGE WEIGHT: 9.7 kg (21 lb 5 oz)
LENGTH: about 74 cm (29 in)
HEAD CIRCUMFERENCE: about 45.8 cm (18 in).

These figures are only a guide because healthy babies come in a wide range of sizes. According to one rule of thumb, a baby should treble her birth weight by the age of 12 months, but this only works babies of average size.

hair of her first few months. Her hair grows quickly, at about 8 mm (⅓ in) every month. By about 12 months, she may be ready for her first haircut – a memorable occasion for a parent. Many mothers like to save a lock of hair from this first cut.

Some babies protest long and loud at their first haircut, and it is not hard to understand why. From the baby's point of view, it must be terrifying to see a pair of scissors approach, especially if you don't know what is going to happen next. Options include:

- Taking your baby to someone who is experienced with young children (your baby can sit on your lap, in which case you will probably want to wear a protective cape too).
- Asking someone to come to your home (your baby may be encouraged if this person cuts your hair first).
- If you decide to trim your baby's hair yourself, make sure that you have a steady hand and someone to hold your baby while you do it.

Posture and spine

Your baby no longer slumps. Now that she sits and stands, her head is more upright. By 9 months, she has developed a well-defined neck. In fact, her spine as a whole is changing. Her entire spine, which at one time when seen from the side was gently C-shaped, is now an elongated S: the neck and back straighten out, while two small C-shaped areas remain, in the back of the chest and between the buttocks.

The more alert and interested your baby is, the straighter she will tend to hold herself. You will notice this when she's engrossed in something. As she concentrates, her whole back will appear straight, though her head may bend down while she takes a close look at the toy or whatever object she is studying.

How bones grow

At 9 months, many of your baby's bones are still made of cartilage (gristle) rather than hard bone rich in calcium. The bones become longer over these 3 months, and other important changes also occur. At the upper end of each femur (the thigh bone, which is the longest bone in the body), a nest of bone cells appears in the cartilage at 12 months.

At the same time, similar clusters of bone cells appear at the lower end of the tibia (shin bone) and in the bones of the shoulder joint. These nests of bone cells are called 'centres of ossification'. They enlarge and accumulate calcium, eventually turning all the soft cartilage into hard, enduring bone.

Sleeping

Your baby's increased activity levels go hand in hand with increased alertness. By 9 months, a baby acquires the knack of staying awake on purpose, even if he is tired. Together with his natural clinginess at this time (see page 118), it can be hard to get your baby to go to bed. This is why it is such a good thing to get your baby used to going to sleep on his own at a young age.

Sleep needs

At the age of 9 months a baby needs an average of about 12 hours sleep a night, plus two naps of about an hour or more each. By 12 months, your baby is likely to be down to one daytime nap, although it may last up to 2 hours.

The transition from two to one naps can be tricky, because many babies choose to fall soundly asleep at about noon and end up missing their midday meal. If you try to keep your baby awake, he may just nod off in his high-chair between spoonfuls. During this period of change, it is best to be flexible about timing and to be prepared to shift mealtimes to suit your baby's sleepiness. An earlier lunch may be the answer. An action-packed outing can also help your baby doze off, especially if it is followed by a hot meal, or even a ride home in the pushchair.

Bedtime routine

Now that your baby can choose when to sleep, a predictable calming bedtime ritual is even more important At 9 months, he will enjoy bathtime. You can follow this with a drink and a bedtime story.

Some parents leave a light on at night. This has advantages and disadvantages. Leaving the light on may suggest to your baby that darkness is scary. According to some research, a bright light may also make your baby short-sighted later. However, a dim night-light can be reassuring, as well as helping you find your way safely to your baby, should he need you during the night.

Refusing to lie down

By 10 months, your baby may decide to stand up in his cot just when you were hoping that he would fall peacefully asleep. He will lie down eventually and, meanwhile, there is nothing much you can do. Just kiss your baby, say goodnight and leave. If he cries after you leave, go back, say goodnight again, and then leave. Ultimately he will sit down, then lie down and sleep. You can creep in later and cover him up so that he does not get cold in the night.

Night-time waking

The chances are that your baby will surface many times during the night. It takes a 12-month old baby between 45 and 60 minutes to go from drowsiness through deep sleep and back to being awake, compared with 90 minutes for an adult. This does not mean that he needs attention from you every time. He may just stir briefly before settling back to sleep on his own, unless he is hungry or thinks that it is already morning. This is why, at this age, you may prefer your baby to sleep in his own room. If he continues to share your room, you could continually disturb each other.

Cuddly toys and comfort objects

Most babies have a comfort object, such as a teddy bear or a favourite blanket, and they like to hold or suck a favourite object, especially as they fall asleep. Parents often worry about the use of comfort objects, but it is absolutely normal, even if it is amazing what some babies get attached to. Comfort objects help a baby to face separation from you, and their use does not mean that your baby is insecure. In time, your baby will lose interest in his cuddly blanket or his one-eared rabbit. Meanwhile, for the sake of hygiene and to prevent a potential crisis, you could invest in two identical comfort items, just in case one gets lost.

Motor development

There are many ways for a baby to be mobile. As your baby's body becomes stronger, and she learns to control it better, she is likely to use a combination of different methods for getting around.

Crawling

At 9 months, many babies are crawling. This is an extension of the commando-style creeping that younger babies seem to discover almost by accident. Your baby's first efforts at crawling may be in reverse, but she will get the idea of forward motion within a week or two. Before you know it, she will be moving at top speed, much to her delight, especially when you chase her. To accompany their escape, most babies breathe heavily, grunt or squeal to show how excited they are.

Crawling is not the be-all and end-all, however. Fluency of movement is just as important. By 11 months or so, your baby will be able to switch between sitting and crawling whenever she wants. From 11 or 12 months she will also be able to hold a toy in one hand as she crawls, making her movements even more purposeful.

Sitting to standing

By 9 months, your baby can sit well and moves easily in and out of a seated position. When sitting, she can pivot around to reach a toy without losing her balance.

She pulls herself up into a standing position by 9 or 10 months, using whatever support she can find. This could be the side of her cot, a nearby table – or even your legs if you happen to be sitting close by. She may also grab at a curtain or tablecloth to help her get upright, with occasional mishaps or even injuries.

When getting to a standing position, her toes curl with the effort. Once upright, she stands with her legs planted well apart and

Alternatives to crawling

Some babies continue to creep commando-fashion when most others are crawling. A few shuffle on their bottoms instead. Nobody is sure exactly why they choose to do this, but your baby can build up surprising speeds on her bottom. Some babies bottom-shuffle persistently and may be late at walking – a few as late as 2 years or more. Bottom-shuffling can run in families, so if you or your partner were bottom-shufflers as babies, it is more likely that your baby will elect to be one too.

her feet flat on the floor. At first she does not take all her weight through her legs, leaning against a nearby support instead. She may also shift from one foot to the other and may then curl and uncurl her toes.

Standing to sitting

Sitting down again can be a problem. At 9 months or so, your baby simply subsides with a thud, as her legs just let go. Sometimes she does not even manage this, so she stands there for a few moments, looking stranded and confused. She may cry for your help.

Most babies are more confident about standing by about 10 months. They take more of their own weight, although they still stand with feet held wide apart, which is all the better for balance.

When your baby is about 11 months, she will probably be able to sit from a standing position more easily whenever she wants.

Cruising and walking

At about 10 or 11 months, your baby is able to walk sideways while holding onto things. This is often referred to as 'furniture-cruising'. By 11 months, she could be using a combination of methods to get around the room, such as furniture-cruising, then dropping down to floorlevel to crawl further before standing up to furniture-cruise again.

For balance, she needs three points of contact, most often both feet and one arm, or both feet and her chest. Her free hand can carry a toy, until she needs it to move to another part of the room.

Encouraging your baby to walk

From 11 months, many babies will walk if you hold both of their hands. A few walk with just one hand held, but some refuse, and they don't enjoy being rushed or coerced.

First steps

Fewer than 50 per cent of all babies are able to walk unaided by 12 months, so don't worry if your baby is not one of them. Girls tend to walk sooner than boys. Parents can get very competitive about their baby's first steps, although walking is not a sign of intelligence and late walking does not in any way mean that a baby is either stupid or lazy.

From a baby's perspective, it does not really matter whether he walks, crawls, furniture-cruises or shuffles about on his bottom. The important thing is being on the move, with all the freedom that it brings. Your baby needs to call the tune. If he chooses to crawl, let him crawl. If, on the other hand, he really wants to walk, he must

Safety issues

From about 9 months, once your baby is at large, there are new safety angles to consider. Remember that he cannot sense danger, so it will not occur to him that a table may be too flimsy to hold onto.

At 9 months, he is able to understand what you tell him, but either he does not remember it for long or his natural curiosity gets the better of him. It is better for your baby, and less tedious for you, if you don't say 'No' all the time. Here are some ideas:

☐ Put away fragile objects, wobbly furniture and long, dangling tablecloths for the time being. You may want to move glass-topped tables too. From 10 or 11 months, a baby begins to stand up a lot and often bumps his head.

☐ Exploit your baby's distractibility. Until at least 12 months, it is easy to side-track a baby from what he is doing. You may be able to lure him away from trouble by offering him another more tempting pastime. At this age, anything with fine detail has enormous appeal.

☐ Get down to floor level and have a look at every room from your baby's point of view. You may notice hazards that you had missed, such as a radiator that is too hot to touch but is perfectly placed to act as a support.

Toys for standing and walking

■ A sturdy push-along trolley with bricks is a good toy towards 12 months, as is a toy push-chair or pram. Both can help your baby to stand, as well as having pretend-play potential.

■ Sit-and-ride toys can last your baby for many months. It is still early for your baby to sit on one, but he can push it along while crawling or walking on all fours.

■ Wheeled baby-walkers with seats are not so good. Although they are designed for babies who are not yet walking, they can be counterproductive. In one of these, a baby can move far faster than he can control, and this can be dangerous, especially near stairs. Even on a level floor, baby-walkers can topple over when they meet an obstacle, making them one of the most dangerous items of baby equipment. Also, they don't help a baby to walk. If your baby is not yet walking, this suggests that he simply is just not ready. In any case, your baby's hips are likely to be at the wrong angle in a baby-walker. He may even have one leg dangling lower than the other, which could harm his long-term development. If you do use a baby-walker, supervise your baby constantly and only let him use it for short periods of time.

be allowed to do so. There is no point in trying to influence his choice. Just provide safe opportunities to practise whatever method he chooses.

Your baby will be steadier on his feet, and more confident as a result, if you let him walk around the house with bare feet, so long as it's safe to do so. Socks can be slippery if you have wood, tiled or vinyl flooring. Soft-rubber soled shoes or slipper socks are better (see also page 127) as they provide more grip.

Hand–eye coordination

From 9–12 months, your baby's fine movements become more purposeful as her coordination develops. She enjoys her new skills in a variety of ways and these keep her happily occupied as she explores her surroundings.

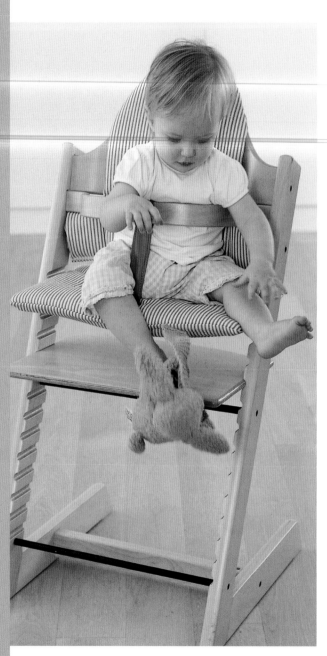

Picking things up

Your baby learns new movements, and her mastery of her hands improves. At about 9 months, she learns to move from the wrist, a refinement which gives her greater hand control. You can see this in the way she waves at people. From about the same time, she learns to use her index finger to point, although she may sometimes still indicate by waving her whole hand.

She also uses her thumb in an adult way. From about 9 or 10 months, her pincer grip is more accurate, so she can pick up small objects. She also begins to turn the pages of a book, although not always singly and not always without tearing them. You should put any special books out of reach and only bring them out from time to time, when you can read together.

By 11–12 months, your baby's grasp is more appropriate to each task. Gone is the vigorous all-purpose grab. With greater judgement than before, your baby now uses only as many fingers and as much force as she needs to pick up a particular toy.

Letting things go

A young baby cannot always let go of objects at will – some of the release mechanism is involuntary. By 9 months, she begins to drop objects when she wants to. By 10 months, she is making the most of this ability. She may drop things behind the sofa, down drains or between a radiator and the wall, but most of all she enjoys dropping things on the floor for you to pick up, squealing for them to be retrieved so that she can drop them again and again. This phase of her development can be trying, especially when she throws things out of her buggy, but it soon passes. It is all part of her learning about cause-and-effect and about judging distance, weight and the pull of gravity.

From about 10 months, your baby is good at estimating distances, at least at short range. She can hand toys to other people and may do so often. She also knows very well not to let go if she does not want to. From 10 or 11 months, she can tease you by offering a toy and then refusing to give it to you, another activity that may amuse her for a time.

Putting things together

Now that your baby has better hand–eye skills, she can bring objects together accurately. She enjoys the sound that she makes, for example, when she bangs two bricks together and may perform this action repeatedly.

By about 10 or 11 months, your baby spends a lot of time working out the shapes of things and how big or small they are in relation to others. She is becoming increasingly aware of what will fit into where. It is fun to put the lids on and off boxes and the covers on and off saucepans. She also busies herself posting things into boxes and other containers.

Drawing

Man is a species that writes and draws, and about now you may see your baby's first artistic attempts. From 9 or 10 months old, your baby can usually hold a crayon, using her whole fist, and make a mark with it on a piece of paper. Although she is not a bad judge of distance, she is understandably less good at guessing the strength of unfamiliar materials, so at first she stabs inaccurately at the paper. This may result in a random mark, or the paper may tear. The most you can expect is a line or two on the paper. Even if the paper tears, however, the experience is of educational value for a baby, and both of you will probably enjoy these early efforts.

Toys for hand–eye coordination

Your baby develops hand–eye coordination on his own, but you can help bring out the best in him by offering him opportunities to practise and refine his manual skills.

Construction toys

Your baby enjoys fitting one thing into another, so he will enjoy putting rings onto a rod. He may also like threading things onto a cord, with your help if necessary. From 9 months, shape-sorters will occupy a baby for a long time. Simpler playthings, such as beakers, also have an appeal. It is also fun putting bricks into a basket or a box and playing with saucepans, yoghurt pots and other household objects.

Building blocks are versatile. Your baby is not able to build much on his own, so he may just place them side by side, or bash them together. However, you can build towers for him to ponder upon and to knock down. The colours also give you something to talk about, especially if the blocks are otherwise identical. From 9 or 10 months, your baby will probably be able to operate pop-up toys himself. He may also still enjoy activity centres, as long as they are not too simple.

Games for coordination

There are a number of simple games that you can use to help develop your baby's coordination.

- **Give it to me, please** Get him to hand you toys, remembering to thank him.

- **Where is …?** This is a good way of getting him to search for various objects and pick them up.

- **Pat-a-cake and clapping games** These are useful for hand–eye coordination

- **Developing the gentle touch** Use soft toys to teach your baby to develop a gentle touch. A favourite doll or teddy often brings out the kind side in a young child.

Paper

Paper starts to be interesting about now. Your baby may enjoy crumpling it or trying to scribble on it. Give him short stubby crayons because he is not yet ready for proper pencils. You may still want to watch over him. Once he knows that he can make a mark on paper, he may try the walls next.

Musical instruments

Toy musical instruments, such as a xylophone or a small drum, are fun, and they help to teach cause-and-effect as well as hand–eye coordination. Demonstrating what to do can encourage him to play. As with drawing, it is best not to anticipate a virtuoso performance!

Books

Books are surprisingly versatile. As your baby's concentration and understanding improve, he will enjoy listening to longer stories. This also gives him the chance to learn how to turn pages. Touch-and-feel books amuse him and build his manual dexterity. Sitting down with a book together is also a way of slowing down the tempo of your baby's day, so it is an ideal respite for you both at the end of a busy time.

Puzzles

Towards 12 months, your baby may be ready for his first puzzle. This needs to be very simple, ideally a tray puzzle with only two pieces, in bright colours to hold his attention. Although it is only an extension of shape-sorting, at first your baby may have no idea what to do with it, so show him. and he then can try himself. If he still needs a hint, you could place a piece the right way up above or very near the tray.

Bath toys

Bath toys will satisfy your baby's love of action. Beakers are good fun at bathtime and help to teach him the concept of 'if-when'. Inexpensive plastic shapes that stick onto

tiles and can be lifted off and repositioned may appeal to his eye for detail.

Although your baby is often happy to play on his own, the best playmate of all is probably you. You are your baby's first teacher, and you can show him how to use things, be it an unfamiliar toy or a household item. Help him notice interesting things too. He will spend ages fingering such intricate objects as keys on a key-ring, or the wheels of a small toy car. Just make sure they are safe for him.

Everyday activities

In reality, you don't need many toys to help your baby's hand–eye coordination. Everyday activities like going to the park to feed the ducks can teach your baby a lot, especially if you let him have a few bits of bread that he can drop too.

Senses and learning

At 9 months, your baby is acutely aware of her surroundings. Now that she is mobile, her world becomes much larger. At the same time, she now has a special fascination for fine detail. In short, she is curious about everything. As she develops, her skills are increasingly interrelated. Her increased concentration and better hand–eye coordination both help her learning.

Vision

At 9 months, your baby looks around the room with great interest. Her eyesight is now sharp, and she will recognize you and other special people from a distance. She is also able to see small objects only 1 mm ($\frac{1}{16}$ in) across. From 9 months, she may spend a long time poking and fingering small details on a patterned carpet or be fascinated by a tiny crumb on the floor. She can now also appreciate more detailed pictures in books.

By 11 or 12 months, your baby is able to follow rapidly moving objects. Only her peripheral vision has yet to reach adult standards. She should not be squinting at all, or tilting her head to one side to see better. If she does, see your doctor. Squints can be corrected if treated early.

Concentrating and investigating

From 9 months onwards, your baby investigates things more with her hands and less with her mouth. She hardly ever mouths things by the time she is 12 months old.

During these 3 months, she enjoys looking at books, and she can follow longer stories. From 9–10 months, she shows interest in pictures, especially if you talk to her about them.

At 9 months, your baby takes her time finding out about things. She is happy to be on her own playing – evidence of her increasing powers of concentration.

However, she can still be distracted if you talk to her or offer her something of interest. This makes her a responsive companion and also means that it is easier to get her dressed or ready to go out at short notice. However, don't expect total cooperation all the time.

You are the role model

Your baby enjoys imitating your actions, especially from 9 months, and she wants to do more things for herself. Sometimes she wants to wash or feed herself, or wield her hairbrush. Let her try when you can. She also cooperates with dressing. She anticipates the putting on of her coat and holds her arm out for you. She may also put out a foot, ready for you to pull on her socks. It is worth taking the hint and dressing the part she has offered because this is an important part of learning to dress herself.

Your baby tries to imitate you if you scribble on a piece of paper or show her what to do with a pull-along toy. When it comes to simple household chores, she may want to copy you emptying the washing machine or polishing a table. She cannot be of real help with housework, but give her a clean duster and she will happily play alongside you while you finish your jobs.

Remembering and understanding

At 9 months, object permanence is well established, and your baby's memory is markedly better. Now she knows and remembers her toys and many ordinary household items.

By about 10 months, she starts to appreciate the purpose of many common objects. She can also begin to understand concepts and groups of things. For instance, although individual dogs may look very different, she realizes that they are all dogs. However, there can be exceptions. For instance, she may not recognize that an unusually small dog with very little hair is actually a dog at all. Equally, a really huge dog, almost the size of a pony, may also test her whole concept of 'dog' to the limit.

If you have told her nursery rhymes, she will now remember them. You can have great fun substituting new words every so often. If your baby spots a change in a familiar rhyme, she will often respond either by protesting or otherwise howling with laughter.

Communication

Your baby has been communicating with you for many months, possibly since before he was born. By about 12 months, however, he makes recognizable words. Although he builds up to this gradually, his first real words are still memorable.

Understanding

At 9 months, your baby has good comprehension. He takes special notice of what you say, thus increasing his vocabulary. He may respond to his name from about 9 months. He also knows about 15 household objects by name. He becomes animated when you mention one of his favourite things.

Your baby's understanding also extends to concepts, and he can understand simple questions such as 'Where is …?' At 10 months, he can carry out simple requests, such as 'Sit down', 'Stand up' or 'Wave goodbye'. This can give him great pleasure. At about 11 months, he may very charmingly give you a kiss when you ask for one.

Pre-speaking skills

Even as a young baby, he began to take turns when interacting with you. At 9 months, turn-taking becomes more obvious, and he happily hands toys back and forth.

He will also show or share things, for instance offering you a piece of toast, or holding out a toy using an exaggerated gesture. This is his way of starting a conversation. He wants you to talk to him, often about what he is showing you.

Your baby's skills are increasingly interlinked. He is interested in things and events both near and far. In addition, he is now mobile so he can use a wider range of things as conversation pieces. He points to

things and grunts urgently, a cue for you to say 'Yes, that is a bus' (or whatever it is), thus boosting his understanding.

First words

As your baby tries out different sounds, his babbling becomes more complex, resembling real conversations. He utters a mixture of one- and two-syllable sounds and copies many of the sounds that you make. From about 9 months, his noises become more meaningful. He may have said 'Da-da' for a while, but now says it more when his father is there.

Your baby may well say 'Da-da' long before 'Ma-ma', regardless of which parent spends most time with him. Experts believe that this is because babies find the 'd' sound easier than the 'm' sound because of their large tongue.

A baby makes his first word at about 9–10 months. Girls tend to speak earlier than boys, but there is a lot of variation. To some extent, both early and late speech runs in families.

By 12 months, your baby makes distinct words and may even make simple sentences.

Helping your baby with language

Respond to your baby in ways that will encourage his speaking skills.

- Make eye contact when talking. This tells your baby that he has your full attention. He in turn will give you his attention.

- Respond when your baby offers you something. He is trying to communicate.

- Don't correct him. Instead expand on what he says. If he says 'bik-bik', you can say 'Do you want a biscuit?'

- When handing things back and forth, use 'Please' and 'Thank you'. This enlarges his vocabulary and teaches him basic manners.

- Use simple sentences. Baby talk is fine because it is similar to the sounds your baby makes, so it is positive feedback. The simple

intonation can help a baby learn language sounds, but don't use it forever or your child's skills may stagnate.

- Make the most of everyday outings to talk about what is going on. Use what psychologists call 'referential looking', that is, when your baby points at something, talk to him about it.

- Nursery rhymes, songs and finger games can all enhance your baby's listening skills. Pre-recorded tapes can be useful, but singing to him is best because he is programmed to respond to your voice.

- Reading aloud helps your child to learn abstract concepts as well as speech.

Emotions

From 9 months onwards, your baby shows a keen sense of fun and a great sense of humour. Together with her emerging language skills, her eloquent body language allows her personality to shine through. In short, you will find that she is mostly a delight to be with.

Relationship with you

By 9 months, your baby has a good understanding of person permanence. She knows which people are the most important ones in her life, even when they are not there, which should reassure working parents. It is important to say goodbye when leaving your baby and to tell her that you will be back this afternoon or whenever. She does not yet know what 'this afternoon' means, but she soon will. More important, she will learn that you keep your promises.

Your baby may still be shy with strangers until 12 months. She may want you close when strangers are present, which is proof of her attachment to you. On the whole, she is less clingy from 9 months onwards, although she is likely to cling tight or want hugs when she is tired or feels unwell.

Even if the signs are changing, her attachment to you continues to be important. Now that your baby is on the move, she uses you as a secure base from which to explore. This is why, at toddler group, she is usually happy if you sit in one place while she crawls away but less happy if you wander off while she plays.

Relationships with other people

From 9 months or so, your baby positively enjoys the company of other babies. Although she is interested in them and smiles readily, she will not necessarily play with them. She is too young to share toys, but you can help to develop her sociability by teaching her the basics of taking turns.

On average, girl babies are more interested in other people's faces and are more outgoing. They notice other people's emotions and show more empathy. At 12 months old, a girl can show feeling for someone's distress, by using a sad look, sympathetic noises, or even comforting behaviour, such as getting close and even touching. However, whatever a baby's sex, it is good for them to meet other babies and children in social situations.

Body language

Your baby continues to use her body to show emotions. At 9 months, she will turn her head away, shake her head, rock or kick out to tell you how strongly she feels. When something pleases her, her excitement is almost overwhelming: she may bounce up and down as well as shriek with enthusiasm. Although some body language is common to all babies, your baby will develop her own special repertoire of movements. As with her first words, you will be the expert at interpreting exactly what she means.

Sense of humour

From 9 months, a baby's sense of fun is usually obvious. She loves having her tummy and armpits tickled. She is also highly amused at the game of peek-a-boo. From 10 months, she may also delight in dropping things for you to pick up (see pages 110–11).

She soon learns what amuses you. If you laugh when she does something, such as spreading chocolate pudding on her face, she will do it again and again. The more appreciative her audience, the better she will respond.

By 11 months, her sense of humour is well developed. She may laugh long and loud at favourite nursery rhymes, especially if you substitute different words here and there. She will be especially amused if you do something ridiculous for her enjoyment, such as putting a flower-pot on your head.

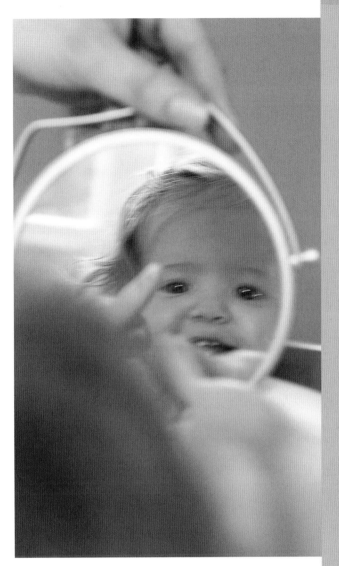

Self-awareness

At 9 months, your baby can easily see her image in a mirror, but she does not yet appreciate that the reflection is of herself. If she is in front of the mirror, she may try to pat it as if it were another child. Your baby's growing sense of self and identity means that, before long, she will start to understand that the image is in fact of herself. However, this does not usually happen until after 12 months of age (see page 138).

12–18 months

Baby to toddler

Major milestones

- ✔ Learns to feed himself
- ✔ Walks unaided
- ✔ Grabs any object accurately
- ✔ Starts to scribble
- ✔ Develops good memory and concentration
- ✔ Starts to become very responsive
- ✔ Uses several words in conversation
- ✔ Begins to show independence

Things to look out for

This half year covers some major milestones as well as a leap in your baby's independence. His first birthday is a rite of passage for him and you. Soon afterwards, he is likely to take his first steps, marking his transition to a toddler.

Physical changes

Your baby loses some body fat, so that he looks sleeker and slimmer. The bulging exception is his bottom, as he is likely to need nappies for another few months.

By 18 months, he is likely to have all his milk teeth except the four second molars. As a result, the shape of his mouth and face look less baby-like and more like a toddler's.

Timing varies, but your baby will probably take his first few steps at around 13–14 months. At first he walks hesitantly, with flat feet, and he may tumble a lot. Towards 18 months, he will be a lot steadier, rarely falling. As he picks up speed with his toddle, he will give every impression of a young man in a hurry. However, his walking may not be elegant, nor always in the direction you want.

Your baby and his environment

There will be some days when he acts like a young baby, but for the most part you can now consider your baby to be a toddler. Once he starts walking properly, he will need his first pair of proper shoes – another landmark in his development.

At first, stairs are a challenge, but a determined toddler can cope by climbing them on all fours. Your toddler loves investigating the world, and this is what spurs him on. This means that safety becomes an important issue inside and outside the home, especially when you consider how fast a toddler can move.

His important new skills include throwing a ball and building things, such as a tower of two to three building blocks. His overall coordination is improving all the time. He enjoys scribbling and becomes creative, entering an imaginative phase at around 18 months. From then on, creative play and pretend play take up more of his time, all of which helps prepare him for the real world.

Your toddler is becoming more independent. He now learns to feed himself properly, if somewhat messily. By 18 months he no longer wants to be spoon-fed and may clamp his lips shut if you try.

He continues to copy your actions, a vital prelude to doing more and more for himself. He cannot dress himself yet, but the idea is there. He cooperates by holding out an arm or foot. About now he begins to take off some of his own clothes, such as shoes and socks. However, he only does this when he feels like it, not necessarily when it is most appropriate.

Your toddler's action-packed days mean that he is probably sleeping soundly at night. He may, however, wake up very early in the mornings. If you provide something to keep him safely occupied, you may hear contented noises from his cot rather than clamours for attention.

Communicating

By now your toddler can say about three words. He knows several parts of the body, as well as his own name. He may even utter his first short sentences, which most adults are able to understand. You, however, will understand his speech best of all, enabling you to have long conversations together. He may babble a lot as well as using real words. One or two words could become his favourites.

Behaviour

Occasionally your toddler gets over-tired and has trouble falling asleep. He may also refuse to cooperate over other issues. Towards 18 months, a toddler becomes increasingly wilful and sometimes obstinate. He may reject his socks, unless they are the red ones. He may also pick and choose what he eats, dawdle over meals and occasionally show no interest at all in his food, making you wonder just where he finds the energy for his frenetic schedule.

All these are only minor drawbacks. On the whole, he is a happy, busy and attractive toddler who is learning all the time and is a real pleasure to be with.

Summary of development

Growth and health

From 12 months
- Body fat content falls, making profile sleeker.

By 14 months
- Upper anterior molar teeth appear.

By 16 months
- Lower canines appear.

By 18 months
- Upper canines appear and she has 16 milk teeth.

Care

By 12 months
- Eats many finger foods.
- Usually sleeps well at night.

12–15 months
- May only need one nap.

By 15 months
- Appetite may decrease.
- May wake very early and want to sing or play.

From 15 months
- Feeds herself with a spoon.

By 18 months
- May feed herself a whole meal.
- May attempt to climb out of her cot.

Motor development

By 12 months
- Has good trunk control.
- May crawl or shuffle.
- 'Furniture-cruises'.
- Moves from sitting to standing with ease.
- May rise to standing without a support, but has only precarious balance.

From 12 months
- May walk if one of her hands is held.

13–14 months
- Usually succeeds in walking for the first time.

By 15 months
- Walks with flat feet and a wide base (the 'toddle').

- Can squat down to pick up toys.

From about 15 months
- Climbs stairs by going up on all fours and coming down on her bottom or on her tummy.

By 18 months
- Comes downstairs more like an adult, but puts both feet on each step.
- Tries to run, keeping her knees straight.

Hand–eye coordination

By 12 months
- Can grab almost anything with precision.

By 13 months
- Can hold two building cubes in one hand.

By 14 months
- Loves fitting things together.

By 15 months
- Removes shoes.
- Can throw a ball towards an adult.
- Can make a tower consisting of two bricks.

By 18 months
- Scribbles a lot.
- Can turn the pages of a book.
- Removes shoes and socks.

Senses and learning

By 12 months
- Visually very aware.
- Can follow rapidly moving objects.
- Localizes sounds very well.

By 15 months
- Is a great imitator.

- Has good memory and concentration.
- Does not always respond to parent if engrossed in play.

From 15 months
- Begins pretend play.

By 18 months
- Can judge distance quite well and see small details in pictures.
- No longer mouthing objects.
- Can point to pictures of familiar things.

- Enters very creative and imaginative phase.
- Begins to understand concept of opposites.

Communication

By 12 months
- Is very responsive.
- Shows good eye contact.
- Understands well, especially if an adult speaks slowly.
- Can carry out simple requests.
- Knows many household

objects by name.
- Says three words with meaning.
- Babbles to herself at length, interspersing this with real words.
- Has long conversations, using a mixture of words,

jargon, smiles and other body language.

By 18 months
- Knows her own name and many parts of the body.
- Has an average of 40 words.

- May make two-word sentences.
- May have a favourite word or phrase (often 'No').

Emotions

By 12 months
- Usually attached to father as well as mother. There may be other attachments too.
- Uses parent as a secure base from which to explore.
- May be very outgoing, or may be more retiring.
- Still usually shy with strangers but may be less so than before.
- Enjoys the company of other children.

- Is usually happy.
- Enjoys nursery rhymes and simple games.

From about 15 months
- Shows growing independence and can be obstinate at times.
- May recognize herself in a mirror.
- Is egocentric.

17–18 months
- There may be battles of wills over sleeping, dressing, feeding and so on.

By 18 months
- May play with others.

From 18 months
- May begin to have occasional tantrums.

Growth and health

At 12 months, your toddler's growth rate is slowing down but there are changes in his appearance as his teeth begin to appear and he starts walking.

Teeth

A child's teeth may not erupt exactly on schedule, but they usually appear in a predetermined order. These are the average times for molars and canines:

- At 14 months: lower anterior molars come through, one after the other.
- At 16 months: lower canines come through one by one.
- At 18 months: upper canines come through one by one.

Therefore, by the time your toddler is about 18 months old, he will have 16 milk teeth and a smile full of teeth.

Now he has only four more milk teeth to come through. These teeth can trigger pain as they start to emerge through the gum. Some children have more trouble teething than others. You might expect large teeth to cause the most distress, but in fact this is not always the case. An active toddler is not always

bothered by a new tooth coming through, even a large one, such as a molar. The only indication that this is happening at all may be a red cheek and a lot of dribbling.

Body shape

The change in growth rate coincides with a change in his shape. His body fat level keeps dropping until about the age of 7 years. As a result, from 12 months on his appearance becomes noticeably more streamlined.

Feet and legs

Chubby in the first year, a toddler's legs can look spindly or even bowed once he starts walking, but it is nothing to worry about. Minor degrees of bow-legs are common,

---

Your toddler's measurements

At 12 months
AVERAGE WEIGHT: 9.7 kg (21 lb 5 oz)
HEIGHT: about 74 cm (29 in)
HEAD CIRCUMFERENCE: about 45.8 cm (18 in).

At 18 months
AVERAGE WEIGHT: 11.1 kg (24 lb 7 oz)
HEIGHT: about 80 cm (31½ in)
HEAD CIRCUMFERENCE: about 47 cm (18½ in).

These are only averages. Healthy children come in a range of different sizes.

and absolutely normal, until about 12–15 months of age.

When a child first walks, at around 13–14 months, his feet are flat. This is because the soles are still filled with fat. His whole foot touches the ground, and this enables better contact with the floor. This is entirely normal and needs no treatment. It will correct itself naturally by the age of 3 years or so.

Parents may also notice that their toddler's feet face inwards when he walks. In fact, both the knee-caps and the feet can point towards each other at about 12–18 months of age, usually because the whole femur (thigh bone) is rotated. It almost always resolves itself by the age of 5 or 6 years. However, it is a good idea to consult your doctor because, occasionally, there may be a hip problem or some other condition that needs treatment.

Nervous system

A lot is happening in your toddler's brain. By 12 months, his brain is two-thirds of its adult weight. However, there is still a lot of development to take place, such as making new connections between brain cells and improving the speed at which nerve cells transmit signals.

First shoes

Your toddler only needs shoes when he starts to walk. Until then, it is best to leave his feet bare indoors so that he can feel. If it is too cold for him to go barefoot, give him socks, slipper-socks or bootees. Choose socks with non-slip soles unless your rooms are fully carpeted. If he slips, it could put him off standing and walking.

Once your toddler has been walking for about a month and seems sure on his feet, he is ready for proper shoes.

- Go to a reliable shoe shop that measures children's feet. He may not need shoes in width fittings if his feet are of average width. However, his shoes need to fit well, although they do need not be supportive – the bones, muscles and ligaments of his feet will do this job.

- Choose soft, flexible shoes that have a secure fastening.

- Buy one pair of shoes at a time because he is growing so quickly.

- Have his feet measured again about 6–8 weeks after he gets his first pair of shoes.

Care – feeding and sleeping

Although your toddler is now very active physically, her eating habits may be erratic. Generally, if she is active and growing, she must be eating what she needs. Now that she is sleeping less during the day, she sleeps more soundly at night – but she may be reluctant to go to bed!

Feeding

It is normal for appetite to fall off at around 15 months, although this varies. Some toddlers wolf down their meals and snacks while others are unconcerned about food, or too busy playing to bother about eating.

Another issue is that food is not just fuel for the body. It also has social and emotional aspects. This is why a parent may feel hurt when a lovingly prepared dish is left untouched. Towards 18 months, when a toddler's obstinacy emerges, mealtimes can become a mental and emotional battlefield.

You cannot make a child eat. You can only make her want to eat. If she prefers snacks to 'proper' meals, as many toddlers do, you could try incorporating some of her favourite snacks into a meal.

Promoting a healthy attitude to food

It is never too early to instill a healthy attitude to food.

- Serve varied well-balanced meals with little or no salt.

- Offer healthy snacks, such as fruit and cheese, which will not damage the teeth.

- Eat with your toddler at least once a day.

- Don't expect your toddler to eat everything on her plate. You cannnot know how hungry she is.

Feeding herself

By 12 months, your toddler can probably use a cup, often holding it in only one hand, depending on its size and shape. She enjoys a variety of finger foods.

By about 15 months, she can feed herself with a spoon. She holds it in a 'mitten-type' grip, all four fingers working as one unit, but she can now rotate her wrist, instead of the spoon, as she moves it towards her lips. Most of the food now ends up inside her mouth.

By 18 months, she can feed herself a whole meal, if you are patient about the time she takes and the mess.

Sleeping

At around 12–15 months, your toddler will probably be down to one nap during the day. Timing can be difficult for a while. If your toddler is not ready for sleep, then some quiet time with you and a book, or a lie-down in her cot with some toys, might suffice.

Early rising

From 12 months, a toddler usually sleeps soundly at night, thanks in part to her extra-busy days. She may, however, wake early in the morning and cry for attention. She will probably play happily on her own if you leave some safe toys in her cot. In this way, you are more likely to hear happy noises and the odd snatch of singing as the sun comes up.

Settling down

Getting your child to bed may be harder than before. Toddlers of 12–18 months can easily get over-tired and find it hard to nod off. Towards 18 months, you may also find your toddler's increasing obstinacy coming into play. The best approach is to persevere with a predictable soothing evening routine, avoiding too much excitement before bedtime.

If your toddler habitually goes to bed later than you would like, try putting her in her cot 5 minutes earlier every night until you reach your target bedtime.

Safety precautions

Toddlers often sit or stand up in their cot when they are not asleep. Towards 18 months, many begin to climb out of the cot. Your child may start earlier or later than this, and it is best to be prepared for it. If you see any signs, such as your toddler trying to put one leg over the side, keep the cot-sides down all the time, so that she has less far to fall.

It may be wise to move your toddler from her cot to an adult bed soon, before she has an accident. A stair gate is also a good idea.

Motor development

At 12 months, your child should have excellent control of his trunk muscles. He may not yet walk, but can still get around and explore. In doing so, he practises what he has learned and his muscles get stronger.

Posture and balance

From 12 months, your toddler has a good sense of balance, at least when it comes to sitting. He can be engrossed in his toys, reach around to get more distant ones, and still not topple over. He no longer has to think about keeping upright, so he can get on with doing what interests him.

By 18 months, he can sit in many different ways. His legs are now longer, and he may sit with both of them to one side. Alternatively, he may sit back on his heels, with his legs tucked under him, if this allows him to play with his toys best. If he then wants to get at something higher, such as a toy on the table, he will kneel upright to reach it.

From sitting to standing and back again

At 12 months, your toddler can rise to a standing position easily, as long as he has support, and he can sit down again with ease. If he relies on a prop, such as a low table, you may notice that, from around 12–13 months, he uses only his hands or even his fingertips to hold delicately onto it, and not his whole arms as he did before. This shows how much his balance has now improved.

At any time between 12 and 14 months, toddlers rise and stand without support. Almost all toddlers stand unaided by 16 months. If your toddler cannot do this, check with your doctor.

Once a toddler is standing up, his balance is far more precarious. At 12 months, most toddlers move about when standing, weaving

forwards, backwards and sideways to keep their balance. However, coordination improves rapidly. By 15–16 months, your toddler can squat down and pick up a toy, and also kneel, without support. By about 18 months he stands up relatively still and does not need to move about to keep his balance.

Getting around

Even before your child can walk, he is very mobile. Together with his muscle power, his growing independence means that he is rarely still for long. At 12 months, he may crawl or bottom-shuffle at amazing speed, even with a small toy in his hand. If there is something to hold onto, he 'furniture-cruises' increasingly easily, transferring his weight quickly from one foot to the other in order to get around.

Instead of walking or crawling, some youngsters walk on all fours, like a bear, for a while. You can consider this a variant of crawling, although it keeps your child's knees off the floor (and his trousers may get less grubby as a result).

Other activities

The average toddler is very active, and his movements are fluent. He can move from crawling to standing, to furniture-cruising, back to the floor to pick up a brick or car, then back to crawling.

Your toddler does not need to walk to be physically active, to work on his sense of balance, or to investigate the world around him. At 12–15 months, he constantly experiments with his body and what it can do, testing it out in relation to his surroundings.

He does things such as crawling under tables and chairs, rising to a standing position and bumping his head, and climbing onto low furniture. With perseverance, he may even get onto sofas and chairs. He does all this with and

without things in his hands. Sometimes he falls on to the toy in his hand, or on to something lying on the floor, and ends up hurting himself on a plastic brick or some other toy that you thought was perfectly safe.

He may also fall onto the edge of a table, hitting his forehead or his mouth. Lip injuries are common at about 12–15 months of age. By thinking ahead, you can help to prevent accidents, but no safety measures can eliminate them altogether, so your toddler needs supervision as he explores.

Walking

Your toddler is likely to start walking soon after her first birthday. On average, children take their first steps at 13–14 months but, as with most milestones, there is a lot of individual variation. To a toddler, being on the move is far more important than the exact method of getting about, so as far as she is concerned there is no rush. Be assured that your toddler will walk when she is ready.

Your baby's first steps

From about 12 months onwards, some toddlers like to have one hand held when walking. Don't persevere with this if your toddler does not enjoy it, or you could hurt her arm. On the other hand, some toddlers love it and, even once they can walk unaided, may demand to have you hold one hand.

One day, usually without warning, a child stands alone for a few seconds before taking two or three tentative steps. She does this with her arms held high and elbows bent, to help her balance. She may not walk again for a couple of days, but she soon will. At first, she moves hesitantly with her feet wide apart. The steps she takes vary almost haphazardly in length as well as in direction. She may try to rush excitedly towards you and end up falling over on the way.

Perfecting the toddle

By 15 months, your toddler can walk with more precision, and no longer needs to hold her arms aloft to stay upright. Nevertheless, her legs are still wide apart and her feet are flat – all the better to aid her balance.

Once she reaches this stage, she will be walking almost everywhere, even if she often takes a tumble. By 18 months, her gait is more certain, and she rarely falls.

She may try to run at about 18 months. She keeps her feet flat and her knees straight, which looks enchanting but is not a very effective running style.

Stairs

If your home has stairs, your child cannot fail to know they exist. Most babies and toddlers find stairs irresistible and throw themselves at them with huge enthusiasm. Others are less bothered. From around 15 months, your toddler probably manages stairs by going up on all fours and coming down either on her bottom or by sliding down on her tummy. She has little sense of danger.

By 18 months, she comes down the stairs more like an adult, but puts both feet on each step. Sometimes she still climbs the stairs on all fours, like a bear.

Different walks

You can expect unsteadiness when your toddler is new to walking. However, if her walking does not become steady within a few months, you may need to consult your doctor.

A few toddlers tiptoe. If they can put their feet flat on the floor, it is not likely to be serious. However, it is still a good idea to check with your doctor if your child does this, because it can mean that her heel tendons are too tight.

Late walking

When a child walks depends on many things, including family history, the child's personality, confidence and general health. Boys, despite being more adventurous, tend to walk later than girls.

While about 3 per cent of babies walk by 9 months, most children begin much later. All the same, 97 per cent walk by 18 months, so it is wise to consult your doctor if your child is not walking by then. Late walking is rarely linked with hip problems (for example, CDH, or congenital dislocation of the hip, also called developmental dysplasia of the hip). Most infants with CDH walk at the expected time. However, CDH can cause a limp, especially if it only affects one hip. Other symptoms of CDH include:

- ☐ Difficulty crawling.
- ☐ Dragging one leg.
- ☐ Pain on walking.
- ☐ Falling to one side.
- ☐ A grating or clicking sound when walking.
- ☐ One leg looks shorter than the other.

Hand–eye coordination

During these active 6 months, your toddler's hand–eye coordination matures as he explores his world enthusiastically. He can now lay his hands on most things that he wants, although he may still be somewhat clumsy. Between 12 and 18 months, his hands may also tremble from time to time when he is playing, but this is normal and soon settles.

Grabbing and grasping

At 12 months, your toddler can go after most things, large or small, picking them up with almost adult accuracy. He uses a delicate pincer grip for small things and a two-handed grab for larger items. However, he still finds it harder to let go of objects. By 13 months, his grip is more versatile, and he can hold two small bricks or cubes in one hand. He can also crawl with a toy in each hand.

He loves fitting things together by about 14 months and spends a great deal of time experimenting. You can help him by providing a variety of things to try out, from beakers to saucepans.

By 15 months, he can release objects at will, which means, among other things, that he is now able to build things. At 15 months, he can make a tower out of two bricks. By 18 months, his tower is three bricks high. He may still like to knock down the towers that you build for him. This teaches him about the material world and how such towers are made, so it is not as destructive as it seems.

Throwing and catching

At 12 months, your toddler still throws or drops things for you to retrieve. By 18 months, however, this loses its appeal. His throwing becomes far more purposeful. From 15 months, he can let go of objects in an intended direction, even though he finds it hard at first. At 15 months, he throws a ball only a short distance. It amuses him, but his enthusiasm is greater than his strength or accuracy. His catching is also rudimentary. Even so, your positive feedback is vital to help him improve his aim and power.

Let him try to throw a ball to you. To begin with, you will need to sit quite close to him. As his skills improve, he can gradually inch further away. With just one ball you can spend many happy moments throwing back and forth to each other.

Ideal toys

Your toddler is interested in many things, including toys that can enhance his hand–eye coordination. These include:

- Boxes and beakers that fit into each other.

- Building blocks and bricks.

- Beads to thread and rings to stack on a post.

- A shape-sorter.

- A soft ball.

- Simple toy musical instruments.

- Very simple jigsaws (tray puzzles up to four pieces), which you can help with if need be.

- Paper and stubby crayons.

- Perhaps an easel.

- Finger-paints (and an apron to protect his clothes).

- Bath toys ranging from boats, beakers and watering-cans to wind-up toys.

- Simple sturdy books to enjoy on his own.

- Books you can look at together.

Household objects can be almost as good as toys. A box with a variety of safe objects to investigate will keep your toddler occupied on a rainy day.

To prevent him from getting bored, put toys away rather than leaving everything out all the time. This will also minimize breakages and minor accidents. Get your toddler to help tidy things into a toy-box or cupboard when he has finished playing with them. His efforts will be very basic at first, but it will help him get the idea.

Always on the go

Your baby is a busy bee. At 15 months, when he is not playing with his toys, he may be taking off his shoes. By 18 months, he can remove shoes and socks. He also carries various things around the house to try them out in different places. Don't be surprised if toys or clothes are sometimes hard to locate, or if you find a shoe in the toy box or plastic bricks in the bird-bath. You may find this trying, but it is an important part of his experimenting with things.

From 18 months onwards, your toddler scribbles a lot, making large round scrawls. This may not yet be representational art yet but you can still encourage him with comments such as 'That's a nice colour'.

Your toddler can also turn the pages of a book from about 18 months. Often this will be two or three pages at a time, so you may have to help him.

Senses and learning

From 12 months, your toddler is visually very aware. She is interested in everything and misses very little. As a result, she is learning fast, and the next 6 months are a time of great discovery. As another part of her transition from baby to toddler, she is putting fewer things into her mouth. By 18 months, she hardly ever mouths objects.

Vision and hearing

At 12 months, your toddler's vision is acute and she can follow even fast-moving objects, as well as localizing sounds well. This means that you are unlikely to be able to conceal much from her – such as unpacking biscuits from a bag of groceries!

Small details do not pass her by either. The intricacies of a leaf, or a picture in a book, can fascinate her. By 18 months, she can point to pictures of familiar things, and this may become a favourite pastime. She may begin to show an interest in very simple versions of picture lotto.

Her assessment of distance is improving. By 18 months she can judge distance well, although she still has no sense of danger.

Interestingly, her spatial orientation is not mature. She can see objects almost equally well whichever way up they are. At 18 months, she may put in a piece of a jigsaw the wrong way round, sometimes insistently,

Stimulating your toddler's senses

Your toddler's skills are interconnected. You can now make the most of her mobility, for instance with outings that widen her horizons. She may find a trip to the zoo very exciting.

- Visiting the park will probably become a favourite activity. Point out things of interest, whether it is people waiting for a bus or rain lashing down on umbrellas.

- She may enjoy water a lot now too, whether it is in the form of a paddling pool, a trip to the seaside, or just splashing about in puddles.

- You might want to take the buggy with you on walks, in case she tires.

- Reins can be useful. They free her hands for exploring and keep her safe.

---

because she cannot understand why it does not fit. Help her by tactfully turning it through 180 degrees.

Memory and concentration

At 12–18 months, your toddler has a good memory. She can remember different objects as well as her daily routine. She also concentrates well on what interests her, so she gets a lot more out of play. As a result, she may not always respond if you talk to her while she is busy with her toys. As long as she responds well and interacts with you at other times, all is probably well.

Creativity and imagination

At 15 months, toddlers are great imitators. Your toddler may mimic you brushing your teeth, washing the car, cooking the dinner or using a computer. This means she now begins to engage in pretend play, a phase that lasts for many years. At 18 months, she may occupy herself happily while you do the chores, if she can have a cloth to 'polish' alongside you, or a dustpan and brush.

At around 18 months, she also enters a very creative and imaginative stage. Give her plenty of opportunities to deploy her imagination. Simple toys are often best, so that she can dream up her own ways of using them.

Ideas and concepts

Your toddler's unbounded curiosity and increasing abilities mean that she soaks up knowledge. Her powers of logic are developing too, even if the changes are too gradual for you to notice on a daily basis. By 12 months, she already understands some concepts and the idea of groups of things. By 18 months, she has some comprehension of time. Minutes and hours may mean nothing to her, but she has some idea of 'before', 'after', 'not now' and 'later'. She is also learning about opposites, a concept that is very useful to her future learning.

Self-awareness

However interested your toddler is in the world around him, at 12–18 months he is very self-centred and can only appreciate his own point of view. There is nothing wrong with this – it is a normal phase in a child's development.

A sense of self

At 12 months, your toddler recognizes himself as a separate being from you, but he does not always relate this to his everyday experiences. While he can see himself in a mirror at the age of 12 months, he does not appreciate that he is looking at himself. During these few months, his understanding deepens. From 15 months, when he looks in the mirror, he begins to comprehend that he is seeing himself. By 18 months, most children know that it is not another child in the mirror.

Your toddler's emerging will

From 12–15 months onwards, your toddler may become more wilful. He makes his wishes known, and they will not necessarily be the same as yours. This is part of his emerging independence, and a natural part of the process of becoming a separate individual.

Individual children vary, but from 18 months onwards you may find that your toddler has an unmistakable obstinate streak. Sometimes he cooperates, sometimes he doesn't. If you want to go out, he may not. If you choose one pair of socks for him to wear, he may refuse to get dressed until you pick out the ones that he wants.

There is no point in having a battle of the wills over everything. It is far better to let him pick and choose over unimportant issues. From around 18 months, you can help by offering a straight choice, such as 'Do you want to wear the red jumper today or the blue one?' Similarly, you can let him choose a book for his bedtime story. This teaches a child important lessons about making choices.

Of course, on important matters, including safety, the wise parent offers no options. Young children need to learn that there are certain boundaries. Consistency is the key, so once you make your mind up on a vital issue, don't change it. You will only confuse your toddler.

Your toddler's limitations

Your toddler may have learned a lot by 12 months, but does not always know what is and is not possible. He may therefore attempt any number of unrealistic feats. The ideal is to let him learn for himself. If it is not safe or appropriate for him to do so, try to explain why in simple terms. He is less likely to feel frustrated if he can see that there is a reason.

Learning about logic

Although a toddler is observant at 18 months, his powers of deduction are still immature. You can help by talking about and explaining things to him. For instance, when the doorbell rings, you could wonder aloud who might be at the door. If you are crossing a street, you can point out why the cars are stopping.

Your toddler and other people

Because your toddler is egocentric, he cannot yet share and has trouble taking turns. However, at 12 months he enjoys the company of others, and you should encourage him to play alongside other babies. He can learn the basics of sharing, but don't expect him to share any of his favourite playthings.

You also need to teach gentleness and kindness. Your toddler probably has several soft toys that he treats less roughly than others. This is also something you can encourage.

If you have a family pet, such as a cat, dog or hamster, show him how to be gentle when stroking it. Even a goldfish can help to teach a toddler something about caring and responsibility. Children can learn about caring for an animal from the age of 12–18 months. However, don't expect him to take full responsibility for a pet.

Communication

From 12 months onwards, your toddler's communication skills improve in leaps and bounds. There may also be times when she seems to be making no progress at all. However, even during these short spells, she is building her knowledge of words and how they are used.

Understanding

A 12-month-old child is very responsive. She understands you well, especially if you speak slowly, and she makes good eye contact. At 12 months, she can handle questions, such as 'Where is the ball?', as well as carrying out simple requests, such as 'Clap your hands'.

She knows the names of many household objects, and her knowledge expands rapidly. By 18 months, she knows her own name and many parts of the body.

Babbling

At 12 months, your toddler babbles to herself at length, using a mixture of real words and her own jargon. She also has long conversations with you, using a combination of words, jargon, smiles and other body language. At 18 months, she may even start singing.

Making words

At 12 months, a toddler can usually say about three words with meaning. At

If your toddler is not using words

Every child is an individual and develops at her own rate. Even so, there is a broad timetable that can guide parents who may be concerned. Signs of possible language problems include the following.

☐ Not babbling by the age of 12 months.

☐ Not responding when you speak to her at 12 months.

☐ Fewer than six words in her vocabulary by the age of 18 months.

☐ Making words using only vowel sounds.

The most common reason for a language problem is hearing impairment, so check with your family doctor or health visitor.

Stimulating your toddler's language skills

The best thing you can do for your toddler's language development is to speak to her.

- Use simple clear sentences. Make eye contact when you speak.

- Make the most of everyday events and outings. You may find the traffic unexciting (or even irritating), but she may be fascinated.

- Use pictures and books to extend your toddler's knowledge. This also helps her learn about groups of things. For instance, cups can look very different but still be cups, even if they don't look like the blue-and-white ones you use at home.

- If you have twins, input from you is even more crucial. Try to give each twin individual attention (see also page 70).

14 months, she repeats the words that she hears. By 15 months, she says about six words, which may include two-syllable words such as 'bye-bye'. At around 16 months, her vocabulary increases by several new words every few days.

Your toddler's pronunciation is immature, and she finds that some sounds, such as 'p', 'b' and 'm', are easier to say. You probably understand your toddler's speech much better than other people do but, even so, most adults should be able to make out the words she intends.

To begin with, toddlers often use one word or short phrase to mean several things. For example, 'kak' could mean 'nice' as well as 'cat', while 'mik' may signify 'juice' as well as 'milk'. These so-called 'holophrases' are usually personal to each child, and often only other family members can understand their real meaning.

At 18 months, a toddler has on average about 40 words. Even now, not all the words are used appropriately. Toddlers often use 'Da-da' to mean all men, whether it is their father or the postman, sometimes with amusing reactions.

Putting words together

The age at which children start making sentences varies a great deal. However, by 18 months, many toddlers put together two-word phrases or sentences, such as 'all gone' or 'da-da gone'. Your toddler may develop her favourite word or sentence. At about 18 months, she is likely to favour the word 'No'.

If she refers to herself, it is often by her first name. Personal pronouns are not yet in her vocabulary, although she usually understands what you mean when you use them.

Emotions

At 12 months, toddlers are usually lively, happy and quite delightful. Your toddler is sociable and enjoys being with you and other people, but he may be less easy-going on some days. Whatever he is feeling, you can be sure that he expresses himself with great spontaneity. All this can be tiring for a parent. Even so, these months are full of fun.

Relationship with you

At 12 months, your toddler is attached to you and perhaps to several other important people in his life as well. Even if he is now less cuddly than he was before, these attachments are no less vital to his security and his growing development as an independent individual.

Although your toddler may not always seem to notice you when he is playing, he still knows where you are, and he may not like it when you move away without his knowledge. Until 18 months, he also plays better and more happily when he knows that you are nearby.

Relationships with other people

By 12 months, your toddler may still be shy with adults who are strangers to him, although less so than before. Children vary a great deal in this respect.

However, by 18 months, your toddler is often less cautious and is starting to become more outgoing. He is now happy to play alongside other children, and sometimes even with them.

Sociability

By 18 months, many toddlers are sociable creatures. However, they sometimes show aggressive behaviour, such as biting or hitting others. This may start accidentally, but it can quickly develop into a ploy for attention, so the less notice you take of it, the sooner the child is likely to give up doing it.

Even scolding and frowning at a child is a form of attention, albeit negative, so the best strategy is to ignore the biting child and give your time and attention to the victim. All you need say to the biter is a firm 'No! Biting is bad'. If he clamours to be noticed, make it plain that he is not getting attention because he was biting. The same approach works for hitting and other aggressive acts.

Emerging personality

You cannot expect all children to be the same. Some are lively and outgoing, revelling in boisterous play. Others are shy and retiring, shunning noisy activities and often running or clinging to a parent for comfort.

A young child's personality and temperament are partly inherited and partly the result of his early environment. As a result, adults who are impatient and demanding tend to have children with similar characteristics, while placid, laid-back parents often produce placid offspring. However, you cannot always predict a child's personality from knowing his parents. As a young child's personality develops and unfolds, it still has the potential to surprise.

After the first birthday, personality differences tend to become more noticeable. This is because your toddler is now doing more and more each day, and is also more able to communicate his feelings. Whatever your child's characteristics are, and whether or not they resemble your own, try to accept him just as he is. The most important thing you can do for your child is to love him for himself, so that he feels secure and is able to fulfil his own unique potential.

Early tantrums

By 18 months, your toddler may be edging his way towards the time that parents regard as the 'terrible twos'. Your toddler's growing independence and negativity can lead to battles of the wills over sleeping, dressing, feeding and other daily activities. When he does not get his way, he feels frustrated, and tantrums can result. Try not to let his outbursts affect the way you feel about your toddler. It is his behaviour that is bad, not him. In time, as he learns to express himself better and develops a deeper understanding of the world, he will learn to control his temper. For now, he cannot help blowing an emotional fuse when he cannot cope with his feelings. (See also page 195.)

To some extent, you can prevent pointless outbursts by avoiding unnecessary conflict. Only say 'No' when you mean it, but when you do, stick to your decision. Being consistent as a parent is vital. Many parents relent and change their minds when their toddler has a tantrum but this is confusing for your child. He must learn that his rage is a waste of time.

18–24 months
Talking

Major milestones
- ✔ Walks quickly and may run
- ✔ Turns pages of a book/draws simple things
- ✔ Understands that people have different points of view
- ✔ Knows his own name and various body parts
- ✔ Makes simple sentences
- ✔ Shows emotion easily and is less shy
- ✔ May have outbursts of temper

Things to look out for

From 18–24 months, your toddler makes huge strides on several major fronts. The most obvious development is in her speech, but she also shows advances in her motor control and her reactions to her environment.

Physical changes

Your toddler is now more coordinated. She rarely falls when walking on a smooth surface. She soon learns to throw and kick a ball, and even to use a tricycle, after a fashion. Thanks to her natural curiosity, she is increasingly interested in climbing and exploring new places. She can also put on a real turn of speed and you, as a parent, need to keep your wits about you in order to ensure her safety.

Although she may still be rather clumsy, her hand–eye co-ordination is better than ever. She puts these skills to full use in playing with her toys, as well as in experimenting and improvising.

Communication

At 18 months, your toddler may say up to 40 words and, occasionally, put two words together in a simple phrase or sentence. By 24 months, she is chatting for most of the time, making simple sentences that show her grasp of the essentials of grammar. As well as knowing many words for the objects that she encounters in her daily life, she can now handle more abstract ideas, such as time.

At the same time, her pronunciation improves. She makes herself understood by more and more people. Unless she is very shy by nature, she is able to communicate more easily with adults and children both inside and outside the family.

Your baby and her environment

Your toddler's growing imagination enables her to spend more time in pretend play, which can range from playing with dolls and soft toys to building fantasy worlds. She is likely to draw or finger-paint with great enthusiasm, although you may not always recognize the results.

She can concentrate well on what interests her. She also has a good memory for what happened weeks or even months ago, which means that she can build on her experiences.

She manages to keep herself busy for most of the time. Towards the end of this second year, you may notice that she prefers to use one hand more than the other, whether it is for scribbling, for slotting in jigsaw pieces, or for feeding herself.

At this stage, she has almost unlimited energy and inquisitiveness, so she is on the go from dawn to dusk – and often beyond. If the weather is too bad to be outside, she may get restless and hard to keep happily occupied. This is when more structured activities and outings can help to stretch both her legs and her imagination.

At night she usually sleeps well. Some toddlers develop trouble sleeping at about 24 months, but this is unlikely to last long.

Your toddler can feed herself, as long as you don't mind some mess. By now, she is probably a good eater, as long as she likes the food on offer. Towards 24 months, many children get picky about food. They can have strong preferences, and they are also wilful.

Behaviour

Around now, you could find that your toddler is less biddable. This is a normal part of her development as a separate individual. She is very sensitive, but she cannot always express her emotions appropriately. She also knows what she wants, and she usually wants it immediately. However, she does not always understand why she cannot have it, so there can be tears of frustration or temper tantrums. A tantrum is an uncontrolled emotional outburst, and it can be hard for a parent to handle when it occurs in a public place.

Thoughtful handling can minimize the impact of your toddler's emotional swings, but it cannot eliminate them altogether. It helps to remember that this stage does not last forever. Even more importantly, there are many positive developments during these 6 months. When your toddler's charm shines through, as it does for the most part, you will find many wonderful times that you can enjoy together.

Summary of development

Growth and health

To 24 months
- Generally pot-bellied with flat feet that are sometimes turned in.

Care

By 18 months
- Mostly feeds himself.
- Usually sleeps well.

18–24 months
- May wake in the night or have other sleeping difficulties.

Motor development

By 18 months
- May start to ride a sit-on toy.

By 24 months
- May be able to use a tricycle, with feet on the floor instead of pedals.
- Can walk more quickly, run to some extent, climb and pull a toy behind him.

Hand–eye coordination

By 18 months
- Turns pages of a book.
- May throw a ball, although inaccurately.
- Can build a tower of three bricks.
- Draws very simple things on his own, using his whole arm to draw and holding the crayon with a stiff wrist.

From 18 months
- May try to put on his socks and shoes.

By 21 months
- Can build a tower of five or six bricks.

By 24 months
- Can turn pages singly.
- Throwing has improved.
- Usually succeeds at putting on socks and shoes.
- May be able to wash his own hands.
- May be able to open doors using the handle.
- Begins to kick a ball without falling over.
- Builds a tower of six or more bricks.
- Can copy a straight line.

Senses and learning

By 18 months
- More aware of depth and distance, and can see small details in pictures.
- Hearing continues to improve.
- Memory and concentration improving.
- Enters a very creative and imaginative phase.

From 18 months
- Begins to understand that other people have different points of view.

By 21 months
- Has some basic logic, but reasoning can be faulty.

By 24 months
- Can hear high-frequency sounds as well as an adult can, but low-frequency hearing is still not fully developed.
- Can easily remember last week and last month.
- Learns to share.

Communication

By 18 months
- Can usually make 'p', 'b', 'm', 'h' and 'w' sounds, especially when they are at the beginning of words.
- Knows his own name and many parts of the body.
- Can understand a total of about 200 words.
- Repeats words, trying to imitate you.
- Can say about 40 words with good intonation.
- May make two-word sentences.

From 18 months
- Speech and language develop rapidly, although children vary a great deal.

By 21 months
- Obeys simple requests.
- May make three-word sentences.

By 24 months
- Uses pronouns, such as 'I', 'me' and 'you'.
- Uses verbs and makes plurals out of singular words.

From 24 months
- May make 't', 'd', 'n', 'k', 'g' and 'gn' sounds.

Emotions

By 18 months
- Is very open and shows emotion easily.

From 18 months
- No longer shy with strangers (but children vary).
- Is sociable and enjoys the company of other children and adults.
- May cry simply from frustration when he is unable to do something.
- May have temper outbursts or tantrums.
- His personality becomes more obvious.

From 21 months
- May recognize a photograph of himself.

By 24 months
- May know his own gender.
- Can be very sensitive (although this is not always apparent as toddlers are also very egocentric).

From 24 months
- May become afraid of the dark.

Growth and health

At 18 months, your toddler is getting taller and looks more like a child than a baby. She holds her head high, all the better to take in her surroundings.

Body posture

Your toddler's body is now more muscular. However, she will look pot-bellied until she is at least 24 months old. This is partly because her back is still curved, making her tummy stick out. Her ribs also lie more horizontally than an adult's, accentuating her middle.

Her feet are still flat, and may turn in. At 24 months, she may also be knock-kneed.

Boys tend to be slightly taller than girls, and you may notice this difference towards 24 months. However, this is a generalization. As always, toddlers vary in size, and there are many tall girls and short boys.

Nervous system

Your toddler's head grows only a little during these 6 months, at least on the outside. However, by the age of 24 months her brain has acquired a complex branching system very like that of an adult. Important parts, such as the speech area, are maturing rapidly. Your toddler's cerebellum, the part at the back of the brain that controls balance and coordination, is also maturing. A part of the brain at the very front, called the orbito-frontal cortex, is responsible for social behaviour and the capacity to suppress impulsiveness, and this is also developing now.

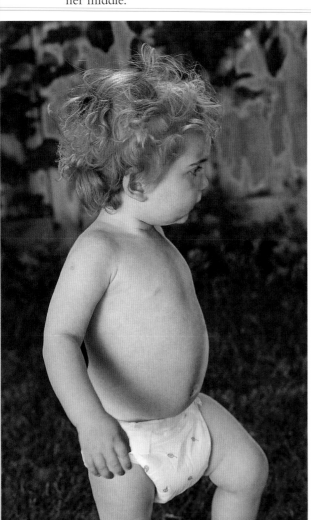

Your toddler's measurements

At 18 months
AVERAGE WEIGHT: 11.1 kg (24 lb 7 oz)
HEIGHT: about 80 cm (31½ in)
HEAD CIRCUMFERENCE: about 47 cm (18½ in)

At 24 months
AVERAGE WEIGHT: 12.2 kg (26 lb 13 oz)
HEIGHT: about 85 cm (33½ in)
HEAD CIRCUMFERENCE: about 48 cm (19 in)

Bear in mind that these figures are only approximate.

Handedness

By the time your toddler is 24 months old, you can probably tell if she is right-handed or left-handed. Until then, she probably alternates between her two hands. Sometimes, there seems to be no fixed preference until the age of 4 years, although handedness probably has its origins at a very early stage of development. Ultra-sound scans as early as 9 or 10 weeks of pregnancy show that a tiny fetus can demonstrate a preference for one limb or the other.

Handedness (also known as 'laterality') has something to do with which hemisphere of the brain is dominant, but it is not a straightforward left/right link. Boys tend to be left-handed more than girls. Family history is also important. Left-handed parents are more likely to have a child who is left-handed. Even so, most left-handers are born to right-handed parents. Twins are more likely to be left-handed than single children, but again it is not clear why. You may be able to tell if your child is right- or left-handed by watching her activities.

- Which hand does she use to hold a crayon?

- Which hand does she use to hold a spoon at mealtimes?

- Which hand does she use for posting things into a box?

- Which foot does she use for kicking a ball?

- To which ear does she hold a music box or a ticking clock?

This is not a foolproof method. Even left-handers prefer to do some things with their right hand. Whichever hand your toddler chooses to use, don't attempt to influence her. Trying to change a left-hander's habits only leads to trouble, so it is best to let a child use the hand that comes naturally.

The spinal cord is also maturing slowly. This is very relevant to bowel and bladder control. By 18 months, your toddler will experience sensations of both bowel and bladder fullness. This is why, as a rough guide, most children are not ready for toilet training until this age.

The number of connections (synapses) between the nerve cells in the brain are at an all-time high at about the age of 24 months. From then on, your child's development involves selective pruning of the synapses that are not needed, along with consolidation of the ones that are needed. The connections that vanish and the ones that persist have a lot to do with the opportunities which you provide for your toddler.

Care – feeding and sleeping

Your toddler is now learning to feed himself. He is also using up a lot of energy during his increasingly active days and is ready for a good night's sleep.

Feeding

By 18 months, your toddler mostly feeds himself well. He can get food into his mouth without dropping so much and is also content to sit in his high-chair. This means that family meals and outings are now easier for everyone, but be prepared for some mess – it will gradually improve. By 24 months he will be less messy and will rarely spill his drinks.

How much and how often?

By 24 months, your toddler could be enjoying three large meals a day – or be picking at his meals and devouring snacks. Encourage him to sit in his high-chair and eat a proper meal, rather than eating on the run. In this way, he will be less tempted to

get up and start busying himself with something else.

Give him healthy snacks, such as cheese, pieces of fruit and celery sticks. Dried fruits, such as apricots, are rich in iron, which many toddlers lack, but they are very sugary, and are best eaten with a meal rather than as a snack.

Milk is a more tooth-friendly drink than juice, but it is very filling. If your toddler shows little appetite for meals but drinks several glasses of milk a day, replace some with water to see if it helps his appetite.

Table manners

At about 18 months, most toddlers enjoy being included in family meals, and they feel grown-up when they eat the same food. Encourage your child to be sociable at mealtimes by giving him a proper napkin and cutlery.

By 18 months, most toddlers dawdle over meals. Trying to rush your toddler tends to have the opposite effect and can make mealtimes a misery for you both.

You can't know in advance how hungry your child is, so it doesn't really make sense to expect him to polish off his plate at every meal. Accept left-overs as a fact of life. Food that has been in contact with your toddler's spoon or fingers cannot be kept safely, and it is much better to throw it away rather than eat it yourself.

Setting a good example is the best way of encouraging healthy eating habits and good table manners. If you don't want your toddler to jump up and down from meals, make sure you too sit down for proper meals, even when you don't eat with him.

Sleeping

Your toddler's days are full, and by the time he is in his cot he is ready for a satisfying sleep. At about 18 months, many toddlers sleep for about 12 hours a night.

From cot to bed

From about 18 months, your toddler may show signs of climbing out of his cot. This is a cue to move him to a full-size bed. Meanwhile, lower the cot-sides to prevent major accidents. This will not stop him climbing out, but it will reduce the distance to the floor. You could also put a sturdy chair next to his cot, to help him get out safely.

Getting to bed

At about 21 months, some toddlers begin to have sleeping difficulties, although this is a problem for the parent more than the child. Your toddler may begin to demand long, complicated bedtime rituals. At 18 months, he may have been happy with a bath and a story. Now he may want an extra story for teddy, a tour of the bedroom to kiss all the

pictures on the wall, or another trip to the sitting-room to say goodnight to the dog. There is a fine line between giving him appropriate attention in the run-up to bedtime and giving in to his every whim.

Night-time waking

At about 18–24 months, many toddlers start waking again in the night. This is normal. You cannot stop a child from waking, but you can encourage him to fall asleep again.

- Ignore minor murmurs from his bedroom. Many toddlers babble for a while.
- Don't give him drinks (except water) and snacks during the night.
- Draw a clear line between night and day. Let him know that he can have all the attention he wants during the day, but night-time is for sleeping.

Helping your toddler go to sleep

If your toddler has trouble going to sleep, you can help in the following ways:

- ☐ Make his bedroom and cot warm and welcoming.

- ☐ Make sure that his favourite things are around him.

- ☐ Avoid excitement and arguments before bedtime.

- ☐ Don't tell him scary stories or let him watch frightening television programmes.

Motor development

By the age of 18 months, many toddlers walk well, at least on a smooth surface, but they may stumble if the ground is uneven. During these 6 months, your toddler's walking improves, and she learns to do other things at the same time. This is because she no longer has to concentrate so hard on putting one foot in front of the other.

Walking on the level

At 18 months, your toddler walks almost everywhere. Her stride is more regular and less haphazard. She does not need to step so high, nor does she walk with such a wide-based gait. She can begin to turn while walking, although this is more like a U-turn than a pivot on the spot.

By 21 months, she walks with longer, more certain steps. If she wants, she can even walk backwards. She does not need to hold up her arms so high. This frees her hands for doing things. From 21 months, she can pick up a toy from the floor without falling. Before long, she will be carrying things in each hand as she walks from room to room.

By 24 months, your toddler can walk quite quickly. Her balance is much more stable. She can also pull a toy behind her on a string. When she is 24 months old, she may begin to kick a ball without falling over. At about the same time, she may also try to jump, but her feet will probably stay on the ground, despite her efforts.

She walks increasingly when you go on outings, but it is a good idea to take the push-chair in case she gets tired and does not feel like walking back. It is easier to unfold a buggy than to drag a whining toddler back from the park.

Upstairs and downstairs

On stairs, an 18-month-old uses two feet for each step. Your toddler may pause on each step before climbing further. She will usually use the hand-rail if she can reach it.

Most toddlers love stairs, and practice makes perfect. By 24 months, your toddler may be able to walk downstairs instead of sliding on her front or using her bottom. When going down, she uses both feet for each tread, just as she did when going up.

Beginning to run

At 18 months, your toddler may try to run. However, her feet are flat, and she tends to slap them on the ground. She also holds her knees straight, so her running is awkward to say the least. By 24 months, her running may have improved, but she stills keep her knees straight. As a result, her running is more like a quick walk or a scuttle.

Sitting on a chair

By 18 months or so, your toddler can sit in a chair. Usually she climbs up, stands on the seat, turns herself around the right way, then sits down with her legs out straight.

By 24 months, she may have perfected her sitting technique, especially with a chair that is the right size for her. She can also move with increasing fluidity between sitting, standing and walking.

Climbing and exploring

From 18 months, your toddler can climb most things. She may be fearless, scaling all sorts of heights, from a chest-of-drawers to the compost heap in the garden.

By 24 months, she is likely to be into everything. This is a sign of an active, healthy toddler. Nothing much deters her, certainly not safety considerations, and you need to keep an eye on her. These few months tend to be filled with daily minor mishaps. In most cases, a cuddle and a kiss will make them better. However, without your supervision and anticipation of potential dangers, some accidents may unfortunately be more serious.

Hand–eye coordination

These 6 months are a period of refinement and experimentation, and you will notice that your toddler's hand–eye coordination develops rapidly.

Ball skills

At 18 months, your toddler can throw a ball in your general direction. At the moment, his aim is poor and the ball falls short too, but he will improve with practice. He can throw a ball with slightly more accuracy by 24 months of age, but he still has trouble matching the force he uses to the distance he wants the ball to travel.

For now, catching is very basic. Playing ball with him will improve his skills but don't expect too much. Even children who later become elite athletes show little ability at this stage, simply because a child's muscles and nervous system must be ready before he can learn ball skills.

Building and making things

When your toddler is 18 months old, he can build a tower of three bricks. He may show great pride in this, and appreciation from you encourages him further. At 21 months, he can build a tower of five or even six bricks, although it occasionally topples over, despite the obvious care that he takes. He holds and releases each object with increasing precision. By 24 months, your toddler's tower could extend to six or even more bricks.

Drawing and painting

At 18 months, your toddler can draw or paint patterns on his own for a minute or two. He probably holds the crayon or brush with his whole fist and, when making a mark, he swings his entire arm. His efforts may be unrecognizable, and he often goes out beyond the paper, but it is all part of his learning.

As the months pass, he holds his brush or crayon with increasing ease. By 24 months, his fingers may grip more like those of an adult, and his wrist is definitely more supple. This means that he is capable of a greater range of movement, so he makes marks in several directions on the paper, hugely enjoying the effect.

He also uses his powers of observation. At 24 months, he can copy a straight line if you draw one first.

consider installing a bolt high up on the inside of the front door.

You may have noticed that your toddler favours one hand over the other. This is his dominant hand (see page 151). At about 24 months, he uses the non-dominant hand to steady things.

Dressing and washing

At 18 months, your toddler cooperates by taking off his clothes. He also tries to put on his socks and shoes. By 24 months, he succeeds with the socks and shoes, although he may put his shoes on the wrong feet.

At 24 months, he should show an interest in washing his hands. He may not always be thorough, but he enjoys being independent so it is good to encourage him.

Holding and handling

Your 18-month-old can turn the pages of a book, but often more than one page at a time. By the time he is 24 months old, he can usually manage to turn pages one at a time.

Towards 24 months, your toddler is also better at fitting things together, whether they are interlocking bricks or beads on a string. You may have to show him first, but he quickly gets the hang of it. He can now manoeuvre jigsaw pieces more precisely, as long as the puzzle is simple. At this age, he is likely to be adept at shape-sorting boxes.

When examining small objects, he often turns them in his hand. At about 24 months, he uses his fingers separately to investigate toys, food or other items. From time to time he is still clumsy or even shaky, but this is normal when playing or carrying things. If he shakes all the time, or seems to have trouble with coordination, check with your doctor or health visitor.

By now, your child rotates his wrist well. At 24 months, he may well be able to open doors with the handle, raising a new set of safety considerations. For instance, you may

Senses and learning

Your toddler goes through important changes during these few months as her skills becoming increasingly interconnected, which enhances her learning. At 18 months, she also begins to appreciate that there are points of view other than her own, and this enables her to understand the world better, albeit not with the same logic that an adult would use.

Vision and hearing

A toddler of 18 months is good at seeing small detail, and she may be fascinated by intricate objects and complex pictures. She is also aware of distance and depth in her everyday life. However, she still cannot appreciate traffic and other hazards.

At 18 months, your toddler's hearing continues to mature. By 24 months, she can hear high-pitched sounds as well as an adult can, although her low-frequency hearing is still not fully developed.

Memory and concentration

At 18 months, your toddler's memory and concentration are both improving. From about 24 months, she can easily remember events from last week, and even from last month.

Until at least 18 months, and often up to 24 months or more, a child can only manage single-channel attention. For instance, she cannot easily cope with new information if she is busy with her toys. As long as she sometimes responds to you even when she

is playing, her hearing is probably normal. Children's powers of concentration vary. Some flit from one activity to another a lot, while others are capable of more sustained play. By 21 months or so, your toddler should be able to play purposefully on her own for some time, although there will be some occasions when she is more restless.

Making connections

From 18 months, your toddler starts to make connections between her experiences. She uses information gathered from several sources, and she is actually thinking.

You can see signs of this when, for instance, she tries to get a small toy out of a beaker. If she cannot manage to pick or scoop it out, she turns the beaker upside down, because she understands how gravity can help.

She knows what various things are for, and she can also think up new ways in which to use common objects. This suggests an understanding of symbolism. She may, for example, turn an empty baby bath or washing-up bowl into a car for her soft toys and pull or push it around the house, making car noises.

Now many of her skills are closely inter-related. By 24 months, she can copy a straight line if you draw one first. Her coordination is up to the task. Just as importantly, she has processed what she saw you do. Research suggests that watching someone else's actions actually switches on the part of the brain that controls that action, which is an essential part of mimicking.

Creativity and imagination

At about 18 months, your toddler is on the threshold of a very creative and imaginative phase, as illustrated above right. You will see this in the way she goes about playing pretend games. Given the opportunities, it is a stage that lasts many years and gives a child much pleasure. It also makes her delightful to watch and to be with.

Her developing mind

From 18 months, a toddler begins to appreciate that there are thought processes other than her own – in other words, a real 'mind' is starting to emerge. Although your toddler is still egocentric, she can sometimes acknowledge other people's feelings. By 24 months, she may, for example, understand that you like some foods that she does not, or that the dog gets excited when a walk is imminent.

Logic and reason

By 21 months, a toddler has some basic logic, although her reasoning is, by adult standards, faulty. She often associates things simply because they happened at the same time. If, for instance, you open the fridge door just when the doorbell goes, and you discover that the milk has gone sour, she may think that this is because the postman brought a parcel.

The importance of stimulation

At 18 months, your toddler is learning certain things partly because he has reached the right point in his developmental schedule.

Stimulating your toddler's development

You can help your toddler by providing him with the right opportunities. However, this does not mean that you have to stimulate him all the time.

- Keep distractions to a minimum. Your toddler can only process one type of input at a time. A lot of background noise is also unhelpful.
- Help him to use all his senses. When you are out for a walk, draw his attention to sounds and textures, such as a gentle breeze on his face or the smooth texture of a new chestnut, as well as things to look at.
- Talk to him about groups of things, such as cars, animals and trees.
- Help him to play without taking over yourself. Initially he may need help with stick-together bricks, but he can then use his own imagination. If he is painting, let him make his own brush-strokes.
- Encourage him to put away his possessions and take care of them. Make this more interesting by asking him to 'Find the matching one' or showing him a red brick and getting him to find another one.
- Reading to your toddler helps his language as well as introducing him to things he might not otherwise experience.
- Avoid over-stimulating your toddler. There is a limit to how much new information he can take in at one time. Over-tiredness is also counterproductive.

Choosing toys and activities

There are many good toys for children of this age, but it is certainly not essential to have them all.

- **Pull-along toys** These are fun and help balance and coordination.
- **Sit-on toys** From 18 months, these really come into their own. Choose something that is sturdy.
- **Tricycle** A child will use this most from 24 months onwards, but it can still be useful now.
- **Small slide** Plastic slides tend to be safer for this age group.
- **Paddling pool** Toddlers love splashing about on a warm day, as well as floating their toys in a pool, but they must always be closely supervised.
- **Sandpit** Sand has many interesting properties which young children love to investigate.
- **Play-house** A play-house, tent or tepee offers opportunities for pretend play.

- **Painting** This can be messy, so prepare for it.
- **Drawing** Crayons and paper offer a huge range of possibilities.
- **Building blocks** Construction toys engage a child's imagination and provide long-lasting fun for both girls and boys.
- **Modelling clay** This is pleasing to touch and handle, and toddlers enjoy moulding it. Make sure it is non-toxic.
- **Jigsaws** Your toddler still needs very simple tray puzzles with large sturdy pieces.
- **Shape-sorters** These can be a bit more complicated now.
- **Hammer-pegs** Such toys help a toddler's coordination, but can pose hazards if you have twins, or your child has a friend over to play.

You can also improvise. For example, a washing-up bowl full of sand allows sandy play, and large boxes make good play-houses. Around the house you can involve your toddler with fetching and carrying, or even simple cooking, such as mixing ingredients or stirring a batter.

Rainy-day ideas

Keeping an active youngster occupied on a rainy day can be a challenge.

- Try using different rooms of your home. You could play together in the sitting-room, blow bubbles in the bathroom, then snuggle up together on your bed looking at a book.

- Keep a few playthings in reserve for rainy days, such as old saucepans, empty cotton reels or a few clothes for dressing-up. Containers and boxes of various sizes are especially versatile.

- Hold an impromptu party for the two of you. Play some music and enjoy a few snacks or a dance together around the kitchen table.

- Alternatively, have a picnic under the table. Turn the table into an exotic tent by throwing a blanket over it.

- Make the most of creative play. You can cut up old magazines and catalogues and make collages together. If you have kept old greetings cards, you can cut them into two or three pieces, creating a simple puzzle.

Of course, you can always dress for the weather and go out anyway. Splashing in puddles is fun, at least for young children.

Communication

The rate at which children learn to speak varies a great deal. Girls usually talk sooner than boys, but there is a wide range of what is normal. By 18 months, your toddler may use up to 150 words, or just two or three.

Understanding

By the age of 18 months, your toddler has a good understanding of speech and can comprehend about 200 words. She can point to pictures of familiar things in books and carry out simple requests.

From 18–21 months onwards, she knows several parts of the body. By 21 months, she may be able to comply with a request that includes two information words, such as 'Put the socks on the chair'.

From about 24 months, she knows the words for most of the objects and people that that she encounters every day. She can also identify a wide range of objects and even if she does not know exactly what they are called, she appreciates what they are for.

By now, she has some grasp of time and understands the meanings of 'later' and 'not now'. She may understand 'on', but has trouble with other prepositions, such as 'behind', 'over', 'under' and 'through'.

Words and sentences

At 18 months, a toddler can usually say up to 40 words herself. She can put them together in a simple two-word sentence, such as 'Mummy gone'.

By 21 months, she often makes short sentences, sometimes three words long. She repeats words that she hears, and will practise to get them right. Now she can ask for the things she wants, like juice or her teddy.

From 24 months or so, your toddler is likely to be chatty and making lots of short sentences. She uses the adjectives she hears most often, such as 'nice', 'good', 'big' and 'dirty'. She also uses verbs, albeit inaccurately, and she makes plurals from singular nouns by adding 's'. From now on, she also uses pronouns, mostly 'me' and 'you', and occasionally 'I'. She also has some third-person pronouns, but cannot distinguish between 'he' and 'him', and between 'she' and 'her'.

Stimulation and experience

Babies who are under-stimulated or are not exposed to a range of everyday experiences tend to be later in learning to speak. In this case, a toddler of about 18–24 months may speak less than other children of the same age and may or may not show signs of understanding what is said to her.

Language delay versus language disorder

A delay in learning to speak does not always mean there is a problem. Often children catch up. However, some have a speech disorder that needs attention. Sometimes children with a language problem are less keen on playing with toys or less able to concentrate.

Your child is more likely to have a genuine language disorder if she:

☐ Is more than a year late in mastering certain sounds (see table, page 164).

☐ Uses mainly vowel sounds.

☐ Does not understand simple requests at 18 months old.

☐ Does not point to familiar things at 18 months when you ask where they are.

☐ Shows little interest in communicating at all by 18 months.

☐ Mainly echoes what she hears by the age of 2 years.

☐ Is difficult to understand by the age of 2½ years.

☐ Leaves out or swaps consonants after the age of 3 years.

☐ Mispronounces many consonants after the age of 4 years.

☐ Sounds monotonous, nasal or too loud.

If you suspect that your child has a language problem, speak to your health visitor without delay. Babies learn by imitation, so the first step is usually a hearing test. Your child may also need to undergo assessment by a speech and language therapist.

Other things that can affect language development include:
• Being a boy.
• Being born prematurely.
• Having a low birthweight.
• Being part of a large family.

As with younger babies, giving your child extra one-to-one attention and stimulation (without swamping her) can help her speech to develop.

Don't worry about a bilingual upbringing slowing down her speech. All the evidence suggests that this has no effect on the rate at which a baby learns language (see also page 93).

Bear in mind that young children learn to say what they hear most often. If you swear or use sloppy language, you may well hear your toddler repeat it later, usually when it's least appreciated.

Learning new sounds

By 12 months your baby can make all the vowel sounds he needs, but consonants are harder to articulate, especially in combination with vowels, and with other consonants (see table). Bear in mind that there are cultural differences. Sounds from other languages are not necessarily acquired at these times. In addition, there are sounds that are easy for, say, young speakers of Vietnamese or Arabic, but very difficult for others to acquire, no matter how old they are.

Consonants

As a general rule, children can usually manage the consonants shown in the box below at the ages given. Inability to make these sounds may mean your child has a hearing problem, in which case talk to your health visitor. Tongue-tie sometimes gets blamed for a number of problems. Many young children do have a fibrous band or 'tie' between the tongue and the floor of the mouth, but it rarely causes them trouble when speaking.

Age	Consonants
18 months	'b', 'h', 'm', 'p', 'w', especially when they occur at the start of a word
2–2½ years	'd', 'g', 'gn', 'k', 'n', 't', but he may still miss them out when at the end of a word
3 years	'f', 's', 'y', but he may still lisp – this is normal
4 years	'sh', 'z', 'v'
5 years	'ch', 'j', 'l'
7 years	'th', 'r'

Mispronunciation

A certain amount of mispronunciation is normal. At 18 months, your toddler finds 'b' and 'p' easiest to use at the end of words. At 24 months, he may mispronounce consonants like 'r' and 'w', even though he can tell the difference when you use them. You can tell because he will howl in protest if you get sounds mixed up. For a long while, a child may substitute consonants or even whole syllables, especially in difficult words. 'Balcony', for instance, may become 'baconil'.

Helping your toddler with language

It is not just a matter of how much time you spend with your toddler. What is important is how you communicate with each other.

- Make eye contact when talking to your toddler. It improves his understanding and helps his communication skills, because it encourages him to maintain eye contact with you. This is important for all young children, but it is doubly important if you are raising twins as they may otherwise not know who you are addressing.

- Talk to your toddler about everyday things. He will respond more and more as time goes on, which extends his experience and his abilities. It is also very rewarding for you.

- Use your tone of voice and gestures to reinforce what you say and to help your toddler understand.

- Try to match your actions to your words. If you are running a bath, your toddler may get confused if you talk about going shopping.

- Respond to your toddler with plenty of encouragement when he talks to you, hands you something or points to an object.

- Try not to correct his pronunciation overtly. Let your reply indicate what it should be. If he says 'bok-ok', you can reply 'That is a bottle of milk, isn't it?'

- However original or delightful your toddler's mispronunciations may be, it is probably best not to make the same ones yourself because this may perpetuate his errors. Most families, however, adopt the odd baby word and use it over the years, and this seems to do no harm.

- Extend your toddler's vocabulary by amplifying what he says. If he points to the bowl on the floor and says 'cat', you can say 'Yes, the cat eats food from that bowl. Do you think the cat is hungry now?'

- Play simple games together. Turn-taking is similar to what happens during conversations. Hide-and-seek helps your child understand concepts. Let him see and feel an object before you hide it, and keep the game simple.

- Spend time reading and looking at books together. It is fine if your toddler wants the same book all the time. You may be tired of it, but he is not yet.

- Use nursery rhymes and songs. These help your toddler with the rhythm and sounds of speech. Ideally, sing to him instead of using CDs. Exaggerated gestures will amuse your child as well as help convey meaning.

Emotions

At 18 months or so, your toddler is likely to be acutely sensitive and very open. She shows emotion easily, whether it is happiness, sadness, anticipation, fear or frustration. All this is part of her natural charm, even if you don't necessarily find it delightful every single time.

Relationship with you

From 18 months or so, a toddler is increasingly good at communicating her needs and wants, using body language and her verbal skills. Egocentricity at this age is normal. Your toddler is aware that other people are separate from her. However, she is still not old enough, even at 24 months, to appreciate that others also have needs, or to see why her needs cannot always necessarily be met.

Even if she is too young to understand your explanation completely, it is worth trying to give her a reason why she cannot have what she wants right now, whether it is an ice lolly or yet another bedtime story.

Relationships with other people

From 18 months, most youngsters are no longer shy with strangers. Your child is more secure and more outward-looking too. As well as enjoying being with other babies and children, she is more at ease with adults. You may find that, by 24 months, she strikes up conversations with strangers and even reaches out to touch them. She has few inhibitions and, in due course, you will need to teach her some precautions before she spends much time away from home.

Self-awareness

From 18 months onwards, your toddler's personality becomes more obvious. At the

same time, she is more aware of herself as an individual. She recognizes herself in the mirror, or even in photographs.

By about 24 months, she is aware that she is a girl. Soon, she is announcing her gender proudly – and that of her friends and family members too.

Fears and comfort

At 18–24 months, there are fewer tears than when your baby was younger. She may still cry, however, when upset or afraid. The world is still a strange place. Sometimes the dark can be scary, or she may panic if she looks around the park and cannot see you right away.

If your toddler uses a soft toy or comfort object, don't worry. She will grow out of it. Taking it away will only threaten her security and cause trouble.

If she uses a dummy, try to limit this to certain times, like bedtime, or to situations that she finds especially stressful. One way of restricting its use is to leave it at home whenever you go out. Avoid giving her the dummy when she is not actually crying out for it.

Frustration and tantrums

Towards 24 months, your toddler is likely to be more independent but still unable to do for herself everything that she wants. This can lead to tears of frustration, and she may flap her arms, stamp her feet, and get even more upset if you try to help.

Avoid taking over and doing things for her. Instead, be patient and let her try. When you must help her, in doing up a zip for instance, try to be diplomatic.

Sometimes, a youngster has a full-blown outburst, with kicking and screaming. Tantrums are increasingly likely towards 24 months. You cannot reason with a child during a tantrum, but you can learn to handle them and sometimes to pre-empt them (see page 195).

Breath-holding

Sometimes, after two or three long cries, a young child of about 18 months old holds her breath. She may turn blue and pass out for a few seconds, or even have a fit. Breath-holding attacks are similar to tantrums, and some children have several in a day, while others have next to none. Breath-holding rarely happens after the age of 3 years. When your child loses consciousness, her breathing will start again, so, however terrifying the attack is for you as a parent, it is harmless. All you have to do is watch over her. As with tantrums, don't be tempted to give in to her demands just because of the exhibition she put on.

A new arrival in the family

At about 18 months, your toddler may soon be joined by a new arrival, or he may already be one of several children. Children revel in being the centre of attention, so they don't always like sharing the stage with brothers or sisters, whether these are younger or older. The age of 24 months can be a peak time for negativity. A 2-year gap between babies is common in many families, but unfortunately it may not be ideal from the older child's perspective, especially if he is a boy.

Telling your toddler about your pregnancy

It is good to give your toddler the glad tidings before he hears it from someone else, but avoid telling him too soon. Eight months or so can seem an eternity to a young child.

☐ Make your toddler feel special. However, don't try to convince him that the new baby is a reward for being good. It is not true, and he will then blame himself should anything go wrong.

☐ Help him become more independent before the birth, but don't move him to a big bed, begin toilet-training or institute other major changes just before the baby is born.

☐ Avoid telling him you are tired or feeling ill, even if you are. He could become upset, and it might make him more resentful of the new baby.

☐ Organize yourselves in good time. Your toddler needs someone he trusts to look after him when you go into labour.

☐ Be sure to tell him you love him. It may be obvious to you, but you can rarely tell your child this too often.

Your toddler's point of view

Imagine the scenario from your toddler's point of view. He is content with life as the youngest in the household, until you announce that his role is about to be taken by a new baby. As far as he is concerned, some interloper is about to take over his job and his home, so it is no surprise that many children don't take kindly to a new arrival at first.

Sibling rivalry

At 18 or even 24 months, the reality of a new baby can take a while to register. At first, your child may seem positive about the addition to the family, until he realizes how it affects the time and attention you can spare, and the fact that the change is permanent.

Many children relish the role of big brother or sister, but others feel more negative. Sibling rivalry can set in at any time up to 6 months or so after the baby's birth. Your toddler may refuse to eat or may develop food fads. He could play up at bedtime, or begin to wake during the night. If he is already dry, he may revert to wetting himself. More seriously, he may poke the baby's face or try to tip the pram over. Your toddler may have tantrums or show other attention-seeking behaviour. Almost any kind of regressive or aggressive behaviour can occur.

How you can help

This is a temporary phase, and careful handling helps. Try to emphasize the privileges your toddler's new status brings, not the responsibilities.

- Give your toddler plenty of attention, and try not to tell him you are too busy.

- Let him feel grown-up by staying up later.

- Show him how helpless the new baby is compared with him. Let him help if he wants to, but don't tell him he has to be big. Right now he may prefer to be small again.

- Avoid holding or carrying the baby all the time. The new baby will benefit from sleeping on her own, and your toddler will enjoy some closeness to you.

- Supervise him with the new baby. Even if he does not intend any harm, he may be rough.

- Don't expect him to love the new arrival just because you do. It will take time.

2–2½ years
The 'terrible twos'

Major milestones
- ✔ Starts potty training
- ✔ Feeds himself
- ✔ Manages stairs
- ✔ Dresses himself and can wash hands
- ✔ Follows simple instructions
- ✔ Speaks so that most people understand him
- ✔ Tantrums may be at their peak

Things to look out for

Parents sometimes regard these 6 months as the 'terrible twos', with some justification, as you can expect some challenging moments as your toddler shows her wilfulness along with her growing independence. However, this time also brings some wonderfully positive developments in your child's life.

Physical changes

As your toddler grows in stature, she begins to lose her pot-belly. Coupled with the change from nappies to underpants, this gives her trunk a sleeker look.

In her movements, your toddler shows much better balance. She still cannot stand on one foot, but she walks well and climbs. During this very active phase, she begins to jump using both feet, although her first efforts are ineffective. She can kick without falling over, and she can throw and catch a ball, albeit with little accuracy. All in all, this is a very active time of her life.

Several new teeth erupt during these 6 months, completing her set of 20 milk teeth. Now is the time for her first dental check-up, if she has not already had one already.

Your baby and her environment

Your toddler's senses are keen, and she is learning rapidly. She develops a sense of colour and can match things of similar colours. She is also busy grasping new ideas. Now she can appreciate the concepts of 'up', 'down', 'in' and 'out'. The notion of time also means more to her.

Together with her increasing hand–eye coordination, your toddler's understanding of the world results in great creativity. From now on, she probably holds a crayon or paintbrush in a more adult way and begins to draw or paint things that represent something – even if the resemblance is not always immediately obvious.

She uses her powers of imagination in her play, building things out of blocks and beginning to engage in complex pretend games and role play. These activities can keep her entertained for some time, with minimal input from you and with no huge expense.

By 2½ years, if not before, your toddler is likely to be potty-trained. This is a sign that her nervous system is maturing. Now she is clean and dry by day, with only occasional lapses. It may be a while before she sleeps without nappies, but already she feels more grown-up. She can pull her underpants up and down, and she can wash her own hands, after a fashion. In fact, she can, for the most part, dress and undress herself, except for stiff zips or awkward buttons. She relishes doing things for herself and dislikes being helped or hurried. Using a spoon, she feeds herself if she likes what is on offer. By 2½ years, she is ready for her own knife and fork.

Communicating

Around now, your toddler develops a wider vocabulary and the grammar skills needed to express her new ideas and activities. It is no exaggeration to say that her verbal ability changes her life. She can make plurals out of singular nouns and can create the past tense of verbs. The results may not be perfect, but she can now make herself understood more easily, which makes her delightful company.

By 2½ years, she is likely to be very chatty, asking as well as answering questions, and keeping up a patter that becomes both more intelligible and more intelligent each day.

Behaviour

Importantly, your toddler's emotional landscape is changing. Now she is likely to be confident and outgoing, although some situations can make her shy and more reticent. She is less self-centred than before and is better at imagining how others feel. Even so, expect her wants to be paramount. Coupled with her wilfulness, which is now around its peak, she may have frequent outbursts if she is thwarted or feels frustrated. Tantrums are more likely when a child is tired or hungry, so you can help to prevent some of them. You can also side-step unnecessary conflict, but you cannot avoid tantrums altogether.

Setting boundaries for your child is important, and consistent handling is a key to good behaviour. Being positive yourself is also important, as it will help you and your toddler enjoy these months to the full.

Summary of development

Growth and health

By about 2 years
- Lower second molars come through, one following the other.
- May become knock-kneed.

From 2 years
- Has less of a pot-belly.

By about 2½ years
- Upper second molars come through.
- All 20 milk teeth have come through.

Care

By 2 years
- Feeds himself with a spoon.
- May become a picky eater or develop food fads.
- May start potty-training, becoming clean before he is dry.

By 2½ years
- May no longer need nappies during the day.
- Now ready to handle a knife and fork.
- Can use a plate instead of a baby bowl.

- Probably eats nutritionally adequate food, although some habits may be socially unacceptable.

Motor development

By 2 years
- Can manage stairs, using both feet together on each tread when going up or coming down.

By 2½ years
- May run with flexible ankles and knees.
- Can walk on tiptoe, but still cannot stand on one foot.

- Jumps with both feet (does not use arms at first).

Hand–eye coordination

By 2 years
- Turns the pages of a book one by one.
- Can open doors.
- Can kick a ball without falling over.
- Ball-catching has improved.
- Builds a tower of six bricks or more.

- Copies a straight line.
- Can put on socks and shoes (sometimes the wrong way round).
- Can dress himself most of the time.
- Can wash his own hands, with some assistance.

By 2½ years
- May be able to unscrew a variety of containers.
- May hold a pencil or brush more like an adult.
- May build a tower of eight bricks.
- Can copy horizontal and vertical lines.

- Can do more difficult jigsaws (four or five pieces).
- Can put on and take off his underpants.

By about 2½ years
- Begins to manage buttons.

Senses and learning

By 2 years
- Knows his own gender.
- Can see very well.

By 2½ years
- Begins to develop a sense of colour.
- Knows his full name.
- Has some idea of his own body image.
- Shows interest in his genitals and may masturbate.

- Likes order in his world
- Can match related objects, including letters (even if he does not yet know the alphabet).

Communication

By 2 years
- Uses pronouns.
- Has a vocabulary of about 200 words.
- Can follow simple two-step instructions.

By 2½ years
- Vocabulary is so extensive that it is difficult to count the words.
- Knows and can recite various nursery rhymes.
- Understands concepts such as 'in', 'out', 'down', 'up'.
- Uses 'and'.
- Begins to ask 'Why?'

At 2½ years
- Pronunciation still immature but can make himself understood by most people.

Emotions

By about 2 years
- Dislikes sharing.
- Is very expressive.
- Can read other people's expressions well.
- Becomes increasingly wilful.
- May sometimes be aggressive.

By 2 years
- Is very sociable.
- Usually very confident, especially in familiar situations.
- Is less shy with strangers.

From 2 years
- May develop fear of the dark, dogs or other animals.
- Frequent tantrums are now common.

By 2½ years
- Plays well alongside other children.

Growth and health

At 2 years, your youngster is definitely a child rather than a baby. Much of her nervous system has its full complement of myelin, the substance that sheathes the nerves and helps electrical signals to travel faster. This development underpins many of the changes during these 6 months. Bowel and bladder control (see pages 180–81) depends crucially on how mature a child's nervous system is.

Head

From 2 years onwards, head circumference is rarely measured because it does not change as rapidly as before. By the time your toddler is 2 years old, the anterior fontanelle (the soft spot) has completely closed. However, her skull continues to grow. The sinuses (air spaces) in her face start forming at about the age of 2 years, when most of her teeth have come through, and they go on growing, especially when your child is 6–7 years old. The very base of the skull, near the top of the spine, does not stop growing until nearly 25 years of age!

Teeth

At about 2 years, your toddler's lower second molars come through her gums, usually one side after the other. At about 2½ years, her upper second molars erupt, again one at a time. This completes your toddler's set of 20 milk teeth. When she grows into an adult, she will have 32 permanent teeth in all, including wisdom teeth.

Visiting the dentist

Although they start falling out at about the age of 6 years, milk teeth are precious because they affect the positioning of permanent teeth. Most dentists advise 6-monthly check-ups for children. If you have not yet taken your toddler for a dental check-up, 2½ years is a good time to start. At first, she will want to sit on your lap, but as she gets older she can sit in her own chair.

Try to stay calm, even if you are not a good dental patient yourself. Most milk teeth never need fillings, but if a cavity develops, it is important to treat it promptly, before it gets painful. There are many techniques to reduce pain and avoid the noise of the drill, but even so some treatments are uncomfortable. Don't pretend that it will not hurt at all, but do reassure your child that it will be over very quickly.

Body

Your toddler is likely to look sleek because she starts losing her pot-belly at about 2 years old. Now her spine is straighter, her stomach muscles are stronger and her ribs lie more obliquely. This all means that her abdominal organs protrude less than they did before.

From about 2 years, however, your child may be knock-kneed, and this often persists until she is 4 or 5 years old. At 2½ years, her feet are still flat, but they continue to grow quickly.

Like the skull, other bones in the body, such as the lower end of the femur (thigh bone) and much of the foot, also don't finish growing for some time. At 2 years, the bones in your toddler's foot are mostly cartilage. Bony nests only appear in the cartilage between the ages of 2 and 2½ years. It is a similar story in the hand, where the wrist only develops proper bones between 1 and 5 years of age.

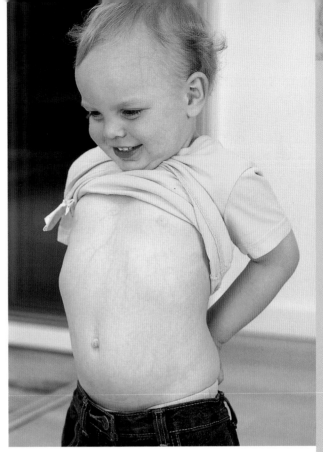

Your toddler's measurements

At 2 years
AVERAGE WEIGHT: 12.2 kg (26 lb 13 oz)
HEIGHT: about 85 cm (33½ in)

At 2½ years
AVERAGE WEIGHT: 14 kg (30 lb 13 oz)
HEIGHT: about 89 cm (35 in)

These measurements are only a guide, as children vary a lot, especially at this age. Boys tend to be taller than girls. Your toddler may be slimmer or chunkier in build. According to one rule of thumb, a child should quadruple her birth weight by the age of 2 years, but this is misleading: it would make a child of low birth weight underweight by the age of 2 years. On the other hand, a child of high birth weight would be too heavy.

Care – feeding

At 2 years, your toddler can feed himself with a spoon. He rarely has major mishaps, so by 2½ years he can probably eat from a plate instead of a bowl, although you may prefer him to have a plastic plate because he may still be clumsy on occasion. He is also ready for a small knife and fork, but still needs help to cut up some foods.

Picky eating

Likes and dislikes are normal. At about 2 years, food fads are common. A toddler who does not develop any food fads at all is quite unusual.

Even young palates get jaded, so your toddler is more likely to go off dishes if you serve them very often. Try to provide a variety of foods. This is important for his development socially and also helps to prevent vitamin and mineral deficiencies. Iron deficiency affects nearly 25 per cent of all 2-year-olds in the UK and about 9 per cent of children in the US.

Occasionally, young children refuse almost everything, electing to live on an amazingly restricted menu of their own choosing.

More varied fare is obviously healthier, but, even so, some youngsters thrive on an amazingly limited choice of foods, such as bread and ketchup.

Junk food

Towards 2½ years, many toddlers become enamoured of 'junk food' and snacks. There is nothing wrong with occasional junk food, but it tends to be high in salt and other additives, and low in fibre and complex carbohydrates.

- Interest your toddler in wholesome food by making it look more appetizing. For instance, sprinkling hundreds and thousands onto a sliced pear may entice him to eat it.
- Your toddler may enjoy preparing his own food. From about 2 years, he can proudly help to create sandwiches or pizza, which may encourage him to eat the results.
- Provide wholesome snacks, such as celery sticks, pieces of fruit or cubes of cheese. Again, he can help prepare some of these. From 2½ years, he could try threading chunks of cheese and pineapple onto cocktail sticks.
- Eat with him and serve at least one item that he likes at every mealtime.
- Get him to help lay the table. He can do this without breaking plates from about 2½ years onwards, and it will make the meal special for him.
- Provide him with more grown-up crockery and cutlery.

Coping with food fads

Most food fads last only a few weeks, so be patient.

☐ Serve your toddler his favourite foods along with a small portion of something different. It may take a while before he deigns to try it, so be patient.

☐ Praise your toddler for what he does eat. Scolding is a form of attention, albeit a negative one, so try to avoid it.

☐ Don't threaten or bribe your toddler into eating. Neither ploy works, and you could end up feeling foolish.

☐ Do nothing special other than providing good food, and cut down on between-meal snacks. Your toddler will eat when he is hungry, as long as he is not ill.

☐ Keep emotions away from mealtimes. Neither youngsters nor adults can eat when they are upset or angry.

Fat and fibre

Fat is essential for growth, so full-fat milk is usually best for young children. However, from 2 years onwards a toddler can have semi-skimmed milk. At this age, your toddler should be having about 400 ml (⅔ pint) of milk in some form every day.

High-fibre foods are good for adults, but can be too much for a young child. At 2 years, his stomach is still small, and high-fibre foods fill him up too easily without giving him much energy. Some high-fibre foods, especially unprocessed bran, can interfere with the absorption of minerals. A toddler can also develop diarrhoea if you give him lots of foods high in roughage. He should have some fibre, if only to prevent constipation, but above all he needs a good mixture of foods.

Potty-training

By 2 years, some toddlers are clean and dry in the daytime, but many don't become potty-trained until they are 2½ years old. There is no need to rush or put pressure on a youngster. Toddlers can be stubborn, and it is best to wait until your child is ready.

Choosing the right moment

You can only potty-train your toddler if her nervous system is sufficiently developed for her to sense when her bowel and bladder are full. Girls often reach this stage earlier than boys, but there are no hard-and-fast rules.

In general, your 2-year old will become clean before she is dry. At any time between 18 months and 2 years or more, your toddler will show that she is becoming aware of her bowel actions. By 2 years, she may crouch down slightly, screw up her face, flap her hands or use some other gesture to indicate that she is passing a motion.

This is a good time to explain the purpose of the potty and to put a potty within her convenient reach. You can also encourage your child to sit on the potty for a short time after meals, when she is most likely to pass a motion.

If it is warm, leave her nappy and the bottom half of her clothes off, to make it easier for her to use the potty in a hurry. Other things being equal, the summer after your toddler's second birthday is a good opportunity to start potty-training.

Sitting on the potty

Expect your toddler to sit on the potty for brief periods only. If she produces nothing,

What you will need

For a boy, choose a potty with a high front to avoid spraying, as his penis may rise up when he urinates. Otherwise, any kind of potty is fine. If your home is on two levels, it can be a good idea to have one potty upstairs and another downstairs.

There will be mishaps, so a plentiful supply of old towels is helpful. Your child can sit or play on them when she is not wearing a nappy. Pull-up nappies or trainer pants are useful, especially if you are going out. Your toddler will still need nappies at night until she is about 2½ or 3 years old (see page 205).

she will soon wander off and find something more interesting to do. Don't force her to sit on the potty. If she refuses, put her back in nappies and try again a few weeks later.

When your toddler passes a motion in the potty, some praise will help, but don't go overboard. Opening her bowels in the right place does not really mean she has been particularly 'good'. Equally, some lapses are inevitable, but she should not assume that these make her 'naughty'.

Toddlers have yet to learn disgust. Some even offer their motion proudly to their mother as if it were a priceless gift (as it might well be to them, since it came out of their body). To discourage further 'presents', be matter-of-fact and explain that 'Poo goes in the potty'.

Most toddlers are both clean and dry by 2½ years. By then, your toddler is also more or less independent at using the potty, but you will need to wipe her. However, some children do not become potty-trained until about 3 years of age. This can run in families.

Using the toilet

Toilets can be intimidating, so your toddler may prefer to use a potty until she is at least 2½ years old. After that, you can introduce her to using the toilet with the help of a toddler seat and a step.

At about 2 years, boys usually urinate sitting down. Your son may want to stand at the potty, but there is no need to suggest it (it is messy!). It does not seem to matter if there is no man in the house to imitate, as boys eventually learn to urinate standing up, from friends or playgroup if nowhere else. Standing up to urinate is tidier in the toilet and, if you have a boy, he may be ready to use the toilet, at least for urinating, sooner than a girl.

Motor development

From 2 years, your toddler's balance and coordination improve greatly. Not only does he now plan where to go and what to do once he gets there, he also puts increasingly complex movements into effect. At around this time, his own characteristic movements and mannerisms may come through strongly.

Walking

At 2 years, a toddler walks well, varying his speed according to his needs. He rarely stumbles on level ground, but it is worth ensuring that his shoes have no projecting edges that might trip him up. This is important because he will not always watch where he is going, especially when there are far more interesting things to look at.

A 2-year-old has trouble changing direction when walking, but he perfects this over the next 6 months. By 2½ years, his feet are more flexible and his walking style is altogether more effective, so that he puts his heel down first with each step, followed by his toes, like an adult.

On stairs, a 2-year-old goes up and down well, using both feet on each tread. He still has trouble standing on one foot, even at 2½ years. However, by now he can stand on tip-toe if he wants and even walk on tip-toe. This is something he does with great charm if he is making an effort to be very quiet.

Running, jumping and climbing

Your toddler may start to try to run at 2 years, but as he still keeps his knees and ankles stiff, it is more of a scuttle. By 2½ years, his legs are starting to become more flexible and he runs a little better. However, toddlers vary a lot.

At 2½ years, your toddler may try to jump. He uses both feet at once and does not always raise his arms to begin with. As a result, these early efforts are not always successful, and his feet may not even leave the ground.

From about 2 years, he is likely to climb anything that takes his fancy. This could be a purpose-built climbing frame or a rickety bookcase.

Kicking and throwing a ball

At 2 years, a toddler can usually kick a ball successfully without falling over. This improves progressively, and by 2½ years he uses greater power. Even so, his aim is still often wildly inaccurate.

His throwing and catching are also better at 2½ years, although his arm movements are stiff and he cannot throw far. Again, don't expect him to show signs of real ball skills yet. He will still enjoy playing with a ball and all the practice will eventually pay off.

Safety

During this active phase, your toddler may be very adventurous. Personality comes into it, so children vary, but it is best to be prepared for frenetic movement and much exploring. A 2-year-old is likely to be into everything, especially things that you ask him to leave alone. He moves quickly, without ever considering risk. At times, he may pirouette madly, just because he can. With unerring instinct, he usually chooses to do this in places where there are lots of breakables.

☐ Always supervise your toddler, especially on playground equipment.

☐ A garden pond, however shallow, should be covered securely with strong trellis or fenced off. Better still, consider converting it into a sandpit.

☐ Keep your home tidy to avoid falls and other accidents. To him, the perfect tool for investigating an electrical socket might be a nail file, screwdriver or fork left lying around.

☐ Always watch your toddler closely in and around the bath. Never leave him in order to answer the door or the phone.

☐ Put glass ornaments and other fragile objects out of his reach. This saves you having to nag and say 'No' all the time.

☐ Teach him to climb stairs well. You can also teach him that certain things must be treated more carefully, which is an important lesson.

☐ Expect the unexpected. For example, he may put his favourite soft toy on the bulb of the table lamp, just to see what happens. It will probably scorch, ruining the toy and probably posing a fire hazard. This can spell disaster on both counts!

Hand–eye coordination

A 2-year-old has nimble fingers. During the next 6 months, her hand–eye coordination will improve further, enabling her to tackle new tasks with increasing delicacy.

Building and making things

At 2 years, your toddler's grasp is quite sophisticated and she uses her fingers individually. She can rotate and bend her wrists well, so that she is capable of fine movements.

Order and precision seem to please her. By 2 years, she enjoys arranging bricks and other objects in neat rows, taking her time to place each one precisely in its exact position.

By 2 years, she can build a tower of six bricks or more. By 2½ years, she has the patience and dexterity to make towers eight or more bricks high. If her constructions did not tend to topple over, they might be very

tall indeed. With every attempt, even the unsuccessful ones, she is learning something new and her coordination increases slightly.

Toddlers like fitting things together. Simple jigsaws become more rewarding, and by 2½ years she may also be able to thread large beads onto a string. From about 2 years is a good time to introduce your toddler to various interlocking bricks, if she does not already have any. Both boys and girls enjoy spending time constructing things on their own.

Drawing and painting

At about 2 years, your toddler is likely to draw or paint spontaneously. From now on, she also holds the crayon or paintbrush with more flexible wrists. By 2½ years, if not before, she no longer grasps the brush with her whole fist. This means that she can now paint with greater precision. She is more likely to stay within the confines of the paper, and her marks are more deliberate. It may not be pictorial art as you understand it, but your positive feedback will spur her on to greater things.

She may spend only a minute or so on a painting, or she may take longer. Although she has more control over the amount of paint she puts on the brush and where she makes the brush-strokes, she continues to be very messy. At 2½ years, a few toddlers are fastidious about spills, but most are completely unconcerned. However appealing neatness can be, it does not usually extend to caring about clothes or furnishings at this stage.

Handling objects

From 2 years, your toddler can turn the pages of a book one by one. Her touch is more delicate, so she is less likely to tear the pages. If she does, she may say 'Uh-oh'.

At 2 years, she can open a door because she can rotate her wrist and the door-handle. By 2½ years, she can probably unscrew a variety of different containers. You can therefore provide rainy-day playthings easily and cheaply.

At 2½ years, your toddler can handle small objects, using just one or two fingers plus her thumb to turn them over and examine them. She varies her touch according to the task, showing that important connections have been made between her brain cells. She enjoys posting things, whether it is bricks into a shape-sorter, a letter into the post-box for you, or a shoe into the garden through the cat-flap when you are not looking.

Dressing and washing

Your 2-year old can usually put on her own socks and shoes, if they have no laces, but the shoes may end up on the wrong feet. For most of the time she can also dress herself.

She begins to manage some buttons at 2½ years. She finds it less fiddly to undo them than to do them up, no matter how hard she concentrates, so you may have to help her tactfully for a while longer.

By 2½ years, she can pull her underpants up and down, which gives her independence when using the potty. She often enjoys washing her own hands, but you may need to supervise in order to make sure that she does it properly.

This is a good time to explain to your child the steps involved in washing. She is more likely to wash well if she reminds herself to wet the skin first, then make suds with the soap before rinsing it off and drying.

Senses and learning

At 2 years, your toddler is exploring much of the time, putting his senses to good use. This is the main way he learns about the world. Toddlers rarely take an adult's word for things all the time, preferring to try out everything for themselves.

Vision

At 2 years, a toddler's vision is excellent. He can see everything that an adult can, including depth, distance and movement. By 2½ years, he is beginning to acquire some sense of colour.

By happy coincidence, at this age he also likes his world to be organized. He now enjoys matching objects by colour as well as by purpose or size. This provides many opportunities to teach him not only about different colours, but also about groups of things. At 2½ years, you may find that the can also match letters, although he is unlikely to know the alphabet yet.

Curiosity

To a large extent, your 2-year-old's curiosity is a sign of his intelligence. At times, however, his curiosity may seem to border on naughtiness. Young children have to learn about boundaries, so you need to teach your toddler not to empty other people's bags, play with household appliances or break other people's things, for instance. However, don't try to curtail all his investigations. Children usually learn from their own explorations.

Thinking things through

Your child's observations are integral to his thought processes. His experiences teach

him to think things through. Between 2 and 2½ years, your toddler still does not have your brain-power, but he can process the information he gathers, and he knows a lot about cause-and-effect.

A toddler's logic is basic, so he may jump to the wrong conclusions, often because two events occur coincidentally at the same time. It may take him a while to shake off the notion that, say, the cat licks its hind leg because it is now his bedtime.

Feelings and animism

At about 2 years, your toddler may also ascribe motives, thoughts and feelings to inanimate things, such as chairs or cars. This is sometimes called 'animism'. He may believe that his tricycle 'gets hurt' when it topples over, or he may say that a toy car is his 'friend'. This phase does not last, because new experiences cause him to revise his thinking. It may, however, be an important stage which helps a young child learn empathy.

Body image and body parts

A child's early explorations of his body as a baby, when he played with his hands or put his feet into his mouth, are now paying off. By the age of 2 years, your toddler has an awareness of himself. At 2½ years, he has some sense of body image and may know the colour of his hair or eyes and whether he is tall or short.

At around this time, your child's behaviour may become more stereotyped along gender lines. By 2½ years, toddlers are also likely to be interested in their genitals. This seems a natural extension of the awareness that is part and parcel of potty-training. A penis, being more obvious, tends to attract more interest, whether it belongs to your own toddler or to one of his, or her, friends. Girls, and their playmates, are also interested in their genitals. From 2½ years or so, children may show each other their private parts. At this age, this is

entirely normal and is simply a part of a toddler's natural curiosity.

All toddlers touch their own genitals, and some play with them more than others, probably because it provides comfort as well as a pleasant feeling. Toddlers often start masturbating towards the age of 2½ years.

Parents often worry if their child masturbates often, or in public. It is reasonable to explain to a toddler that this is something that is done at home, not in public – a matter once again of boundaries. However, you should not try to stop your child masturbating altogether, nor will you succeed. Scolding only makes a child feel worse about it. If your toddler masturbates a lot, look instead for a cause of tension or insecurity that might be increasing his need for comfort.

Concentration, memory and imagination

As your toddler's concentration and memory skills improve, she is able to make more connections and expand her learning base. Watching her increasingly imaginative play is a delight.

Concentration and memory

At 2 years, a toddler can concentrate well, and her attention gradually becomes less one-channel. However, this depends on what she is doing and how interesting she finds it.

Your toddler can remember well, which enables her to build on her knowledge. By 2 years, she probably knows her own gender. At 2½ years, she knows her full name. She also knows several nursery rhymes and can recite them unprompted. She certainly notices if you substitute one or more words, and she may protest loudly until you correct yourself.

By 2½ years, she has also learned many important concepts, such as 'in', 'out', 'down', 'up', 'before' and 'after'. She now begins to have a better grasp of space and time.

Imagination in play

From 2 years, your toddler engages increasingly in imaginative play. She has a good grasp of symbolism – in other words, that one thing (such as an empty drawer) can represent other things (such as a doll's bed). Toys need not be complicated to stretch her mind. Simple toys are often best. The more active the toy, the more passive is the child.

She may be holding tea-parties for her soft toys or dolls. Boys of about 2 years often play with dolls too. This is completely normal and nothing to worry about. Toddlers often feel the need for a companion, and fantasy play is valuable for both sexes. It also helps them to learn how to be gentle and show affection.

By 2½ years, creative and imaginative play take up much of your toddler's time. Her improved hand–eye coordination means that she starts to become more visibly creative. She enjoys painting, drawing and making things. Textures are important at this age, so finger-paints and modelling clay have a special appeal.

Television

At about 2 years, toddlers can become entranced by television and videos. The debate continues as to exactly how television can harm a young child, but there is little doubt that exposure in the early years can have lasting effects on the growing brain and body.

Research from the USA suggests that prolonged viewing between the ages of 1 and 3 years is linked with attention deficit hyperactivity disorder (ADHD). There is also evidence to suggest that 6- to 10-year-old children who watch violent scenes and identify with aggressive characters tend to become angry, violent adults.

Extensive viewing can affect a child's posture and overall activity levels. It has also been linked with obesity, partly because, in many households, snacking goes hand in hand with viewing. It may also be because watching television uses up even fewer calories than sitting doing nothing.

However, probably the most compelling reason is that too much television can interfere with a child getting out and about, taking exercise, learning language and developing social skills.

- From 2–3 years, around 30 minutes a day is probably enough. Television is a passive medium and your child may become almost unbearably active later in the day if she spends too long glued to the screen.

- Each day, with your child, try to select in advance one or two programmes that she wants to watch and that you are happy to let her view.

- Watch with your toddler whenever you can. This makes it a shared experience that you can talk about later. It is also easier to distract her with some other activity when it is time to switch off the television.

- Don't install a television set in her bedroom. Many parents come to regret this.

Communication

These 6 months see a huge growth in your child's ability to communicate. His blossoming language skills match his development in other areas, enabling him to express his ideas and interests, and driving him forwards into new pursuits.

Understanding

At about 2 years, your toddler may be able to follow a simple two-step instruction, such as 'Bring the socks to me and the shoes to Daddy'. By 2½ years, he can probably understand most of what you say. From now on, if you don't want him to know about something, don't say it in front of him, even if he appears not to be listening.

Speaking

A 2-year-old toddler has a vocabulary of about 200 words, covering many common objects. By 2½ years, he knows and uses so many words that it is almost impossible to keep track of them. Even so, he may occasionally misapply words, or generalize from those that he knows. For example, he may use 'apple' for any round fruit.

At 2½ years, your toddler makes plurals out of singular nouns by adding 's', and he can create the past tense of verbs by adding the suffix '-ed'. The result is not always perfect, but most people understand 'sheeps' and 'eated'. He also uses the personal pronouns 'I', 'me', 'you', 'him', 'her', and even 'he' and 'she'.

At 2 years, he knows what 'today' means. By 2½ years, he probably understands 'tomorrow', and he has words for more abstract ideas too. Now he also uses the word 'and'.

His sentences may still be only about three words long, but they convey more complex meaning. From 2½ years onwards, he may be offering a running commentary on what he is doing, whether it is going to the toilet or looking in the garden shed. He is capable of telling you what he is going to do now, and also what he plans to do next. Thus his language ability and his thought processes go hand in hand.

Pronunciation

Your toddler learns new words and their pronunciation by repeating what you say, even when he does not know what the words mean. This repetition is sometimes referred to as 'echolalia', and it is normal from the age of about 14 months until 3 years or so.

His pronunciation will still be immature. For example, at 2 or even 2½ years, he is likely to leave out the final consonant of a word. The best way to help is not to correct him overtly, but to repeat the word, pronouncing it correctly, in a longer or more complex sentence.

If a word has two consecutive consonants, a 2-year-old often omits one of them. Even so, most of the time he can make himself understood because of the other words in the sentence and because of the lively rhythm of his speech. If his voice is flat or has a nasal tone, he may have a hearing problem or a speech disorder.

Toddlers often show an appreciation of sounds and rhythm. From the age of 2 years, your child may become interested in hearing snatches of music other than nursery rhymes. He sings along with the radio, or sometimes just to himself, by the age of 2½ years.

Conversations

From 2 years onwards, your toddler is probably excellent company. He has immense charm, due partly to the development of his conversational skills. At 2 years, a toddler is usually highly expressive and enjoys interacting with you and other adults.

From about 2½ years, your toddler knows the word 'why', and begins to use it lavishly. He is responsive, and he expects you to be too. Children vary, but on the whole this is a chatty time. Your toddler will probably ask a lot of questions and hold long and increasingly stimulating conversations with you. He knows many of the social rules of conversation, although he will still interrupt adults, especially when he is excited. His world is enthralling and immediate. He cannot necessarily understand when you are tired or busy. You cannot always drop everything to attend to his enquiries, but you can keep any promises you make to explain something later.

Emotions

A 2-year-old is an attractive soul, expressive and brimming with personality. She is lively, sociable and happy for most of the time. However, you cannot expect her to be all sweetness and light, and during these 6 months some moments can pose more of a challenge. Remember that, if your child is sometimes delightful, then that is her true nature. All you need to do is bring out the best in her.

Confidence and sociability

From 2 years, your toddler is likely to be confident and less shy. She is more outgoing, even with strangers. Depending on her personality, she may strike up conversations with them. She is completely at ease in familiar situations, although she may hang back or even run to your side for comfort in some circumstances.

Some children are more reticent, even at 2½ years, and rarely show their sociable side. Perhaps your toddler is shy at first meeting someone, but then opens up. If your child is communicative in a familiar setting then all is likely to be well. However, talk to your health visitor if you are concerned.

Expressing and reading moods and feelings

Your toddler at 2 years is very expressive, showing her feelings easily, and this continues for at least the next 6–12 months. Even before she says a word, you will know how she feels from the glee in her eyes, the down-turn of her lips or the angle at which she holds her head.

From now on, your toddler is also good at reading other people's emotions. Girls tend to be better at this than boys, although there are no hard-and-fast rules. The important thing is that, from about 2 years, your child begins to appreciate that other people also have needs. She is beginning to imagine how they might feel, but she has some way to go. That's why she still regards her own needs and wants as foremost, and often urgent. A 2-year old is not good at waiting, although you may see signs of improvement by 2½ years.

You can help your toddler to appreciate other people's viewpoints by explaining to her how they might feel. Use simple words, such as 'sad' and 'happy', to talk about those emotions. You can extend this to characters in her books. For instance, when you are reading together, you could point out to her that the little girl in the picture is sad because her dog is lost.

Increasing independence

From 2 years or so, your toddler is more capable than ever, and she is likely to want to do everything herself. This is not always feasible, so expect her to feel frustrated at times.

Wilfulness and negativity tend to peak towards the age of 2½ years. Much of your toddler's negative streak is a necessary part of her becoming independent from you.

If you can, leave her to work things out herself. If not, draw on your reserves of tact and diplomacy to help her. 'Maybe you can do it next time' is much more encouraging than pointing out that she will not manage her zip no matter how hard she tugs at it.

Your toddler also wants to do things when she wants to. It can be hard to reason with someone so insistent, especially if she is on the brink of an outburst, but luckily at 2½ years, she can still be distracted. You can make use of this to lure her away from something you would rather she didn't do and point her in the direction of another pursuit that you find more acceptable.

Some toddlers get to the point of deliberate non-cooperation. This is because they are testing the parent to find out how far they can go. It is up to you to set the limits, not your child. For instance, if you ask your toddler to tidy her toys or get undressed for a bath, she may dig in her heels. Fortunately, you are older and smarter. You can sometimes win her over by turning it into a game and saying 'I bet you can't put your bricks away in the box before I put the books away'.

You can take turns doing simple tasks, for instance each of you tidying one toy away. Your toddler may also be more keen to do things if you explain that this is what big boys and girls do. Few 2-year-olds can resist the thrill of being 'big'.

Difficult behaviour

Despite your toddler's growing independence, he is not yet emotionally mature. There is much you can do to teach him about discipline and lessen the impact of his emotional outbursts.

Behaviour and boundaries

Discipline is an ugly word, but all it means is learning to behave in an acceptable way. Children have to learn this, just as you must learn to conform to the rules in, say, a new workplace.

Apart from setting a good example yourself, the best way of teaching your child discipline is to set reasonable boundaries. In this way, your 2-year-old will eventually learn right from wrong. Two years is not too early to start.

Improving his behaviour

There are some guidelines you can follow to help you cope with your child's actions.

☐ Consistency is important. For instance, if you don't want your child to play football in the living-room, don't relax the rule just because old friends are visiting.

☐ Praise your toddler for what he does right. Being positive always helps.

☐ Instead of saying 'No' and 'Don't' all the time, use positive phrases. 'Walking on the pavement is safer' sounds more encouraging than 'Don't walk in the road'.

☐ When your child does something wrong, explain why he should not do it again. If he continues, say 'No' and remove him swiftly from the situation. He has to learn when you mean 'No'.

☐ Don't scold or scream at him. He values negative attention more than no attention at all. Interestingly, this behaviour has been demonstrated in laboratory rats, who prefer to get an electric shock rather than no reaction at all.

Aggression

From about 2 years, your toddler may play with other children, but he is still more likely to play alongside them rather than with them. One reason is that sharing is still an alien concept. By 2½ years, he plays well in the company of others, but don't expect him to make lasting friends yet.

The odd show of aggression is normal from about 2 years, especially when a playmate helps herself to his favourite toy. However, a swipe at another toddler, or even a kick, does not mean that your child has violent tendencies, although more persistent aggressive behaviour can be significant.

If your child lashes out, it is best to pay attention to the victim rather than the aggressor, which tends to be counter productive. Above all, don't lose your temper. If your child bites another child (or bites you, as sometimes happens), don't ever bite him back. Some parents advocate this, but it can be cruel, and it does not work. The only lesson the child learns is that using violence is acceptable.

Dealing with tantrums

First, rest assured that all toddlers have tantrums and that, as a parent, it is not your fault. Most 2-year-olds have at least one tantrum a week, and some have more. Tantrums occur when a child is frustrated or enraged and can find no other outlet. Your toddler wants something now, and he cannot understand why he cannot have it. As a result, he screams, kicks, stamps his feet and even flings himself dramatically to the ground.

You can help to prevent tantrums by staying firm on important issues and letting go on minor matters. Make clear that some issues are not open to negotiation, such as playing with the knobs on the oven or opening the car door. On the other hand, which T-shirt he chooses to wear today hardly matters. You can also make sure your child does not get too hungry or over-tired, as these are times when outbursts are more likely.

If (or when) your child has a tantrum, make sure that he comes to no harm. You are the adult, so stay calm. If you are at home, try ignoring him and getting on with something else. His dramatic display will lose its purpose if there is no audience.

Smacking him will not help. Reasoning with him is a waste of breath at this point because he will not be receptive. He is, literally, beside himself during a tantrum. The use of force won't help him, and in any case smacking is cruel.

Above all, don't give in. If you refused to give him an ice-cream before the tantrum, don't give him one afterwards. He must learn that his outbursts are pointless.

2$^1\!/_2$–3 years
Caring and sharing

Major milestones

✔ May become dry at nights

✔ Walks and runs well/learns to ride a tricycle

✔ Knows colours and understands groups of things

✔ Thinks more logically

✔ Engages in long conversations using extensive vocabulary

✔ Becomes interested in other children

✔ Learns to share

Things to look out for

From 2½ to 3 years is a lively, happy time, during which your toddler becomes more grown-up while losing none of her baby appeal. She is amusing but at the same time almost sensible, and she is excellent company, whether or not you are with her for most of the day. It is staggering to think how far she has progressed in 3 years.

Physical changes

During these 6 months, her movements become more accurate and more coordinated. She walks and runs well, and uses stairs much like an adult, although she will not be as careful, especially when she is in a hurry. Now she can work out what the pedals on her tricycle actually do. She makes more complex structures out of her building blocks, and these too turn into fantasy play.

Your child and her environment

Towards the age of 3 years, your toddler is in many ways maturing into a child. She has made huge strides in logical thinking and understanding, and is now much more aware of other people's feelings and moods. For one thing, this makes her far more caring than before.

She is sociable and can take turns when necessary. She is also happy to share at least some of her belongings with other children. As a result, she may well play *with* them, rather than alongside them as she did when she was younger. When this starts to happen, she is on her way to making real friends outside the family.

At this age, your toddler feeds herself well, wielding her own knife and fork unless the food is difficult to cut. Toddlers' appetites vary, but they often eat a balanced diet, apart from the odd likes and dislikes. Your toddler is probably a good sleeper now, although she may talk in her sleep. Some toddlers have the occasional nightmare, but most pass quite quickly through this phase to enjoy peaceful nights.

Communicating

Your toddler can understand almost everything you say, and she constantly wants to know more. This means that you can now begin to reason with her on many issues. It also means that, by the time she is 3 years old, most of her questions will begin with 'Why'. Toddlers at this age are usually very

talkative, and she will probably give you a running commentary on her activities, whether or not you ask for one.

She may begin to count towards the age of 3 years, or at least to repeat three or more numbers after you. Her speech is fluent and expressive, with a large vocabulary. Despite imperfect grammar, she is very articulate and can easily make herself understood. In short, her speech is enchanting.

Behaviour

Your toddler now concentrates well. Instead of flitting from one activity to the next, she spends a long time amusing herself with her toys. She is also very creative and draws spontaneously, exercising her vivid imagination. The world of make-believe takes up a lot of her day, whether she is dressing up or playing house.

Her manual dexterity shows when she is dressing or undressing herself. She may not always be very quick, but by the age of 3 years she can manage almost all her clothes and shoes, including some buttons. Understandably, shoelaces and other fiddly fastenings are still likely to baffle her.

Her independence extends to her toilet habits. Toddlers are often clean and dry in the daytime by 2½ years, and some become dry at night by their third birthday. Be patient if your toddler is not dry yet – she soon will be. Now she may use a toilet during the day instead of a potty. Apart from needing help with wiping and hand-washing, she is self-sufficient at dealing with her bowels and bladder.

Along with her sociability, your toddler's independence means that she is now ready to spend more time outside the home, enjoying new experiences, without you by her side. You will probably be considering nursery school or playgroup for your child towards the age of 3 years. Spending several hours a day in a different environment can stimulate your toddler and enrich her learning.

Summary of development

Growth and health

By 2½ years
• The immune system continues to mature.
• Frequent infections are normal.

From 2½ years
• Face and body look more like a child's.

Care

By 2½ years
• May be clean and dry by day.

From 2½ years
• Appetite likely to be good, but still has some strong likes and dislikes.
• Can feed himself using a knife and fork, and eats from plate instead of baby bowl.

By about 3 years
• May be dry at night.
• May be using toilet more often than potty.
• Is independent in his toilet habits, except for wiping.

Motor development

By 2½ years
• Balance is good.
• Walks well with adult type of gait.

By 3 years
• Muscles are better developed.
• Can now stand on one foot for a few seconds.
• Can manage to go up stairs with one foot on each step (but still uses two feet on each step coming down).
• May go up and down stairs relatively quickly.
• May jump off bottom step.
• Climbs well and may be adventurous.
• Rides his tricycle using the pedals.
• Likely to run well.
• Can jump better.

Hand–eye coordination

By 3 years
• Kicks a ball more accurately.
• Can now throw a ball without losing his balance.
• Holds a pencil or crayon like an adult.
• Draws spontaneously.
• Can draw basic enclosed shapes and simple figures.
• Can copy a circle.
• Can mostly dress and undress himself.
• Can manage some buttons but not shoelaces.

Senses and learning

By 2¹/₂ years
- Enjoys playing on his own.
- Has a good memory.
- Understands pairs and groups of things such as animals, clothes, buildings and vehicles.
- Can match related objects, such as a cup and saucer, socks and shoes, brush and comb.
- Has some colour sense and knows some colours.
- Knows his full name and his gender.

From about 2¹/₂ years
- Can concentrate well instead of leaping from one activity to another.
- Is very imaginative and creative.
- Has increasing powers of logical thinking.

By 3 years
- Knows many colours.
- May know his age.

From about 3 years
- May recognize some letters.
- May be able to count up to five.
- Can be reasoned with, at least some of the time.

Communication

By 2¹/₂ years
- Has extensive vocabulary, including the word 'and'.
- Uses the words 'today' and 'tomorrow'.
- Can make himself understood by most people although his pronunciation is still immature.
- Can remember and recite nursery rhymes.

From 2¹/₂ years
- May give a run-down of his activities.

By about 3 years
- Can understand almost everything you say.
- Understands and uses the word 'yesterday'.
- May know the days of the week.
- Asks 'why' a lot.
- Can make five-word sentences.

From 3 years
- May want to know where babies come from.

Emotions

From 2¹/₂ years
- More interested in other people and what they think or feel.
- Interested in his place within the family and his relationship to others.
- Talks to adults, including strangers, without much shyness.
- May develop some fears or phobias.
- Tantrums become less frequent.
- Is increasingly independent.
- Is less self-centred.

Towards 3 years
- May enjoy looking at himself in the mirror.

By about 3 years
- Learns to share with other children.
- Learns to take turns.

From 3 years
- Starts to make friends outside the family.

Growth and health

Your toddler is still growing rapidly and her proportions are changing. Towards the age of 3 years, many children seem to grow in fits and starts. You will probably notice times when your toddler seems to outgrow many clothes all at once, following by lulls when her size seems static for weeks, or even months.

Bone growth and length

At about 2½ years, your toddler's long bones, such as her thighs and shins, are lengthening rapidly. Coupled with a decrease in her body's fat content, this changes the appearance of her overall shape.

Even so, many bones are still mostly cartilage. It is not until she is 3 years old that the top end of her fibula (the outer bone of the shin) starts growing calcified bone. This is why, when a toddler or young child breaks a bone, it is often a 'greenstick' fracture, which means that the break does not go right through the bone.

Your toddler's measurements

At 2½ years
AVERAGE WEIGHT: 14 kg (30 lb 13 oz)
HEIGHT: about 89 cm (35 in)

At 3 years
AVERAGE WEIGHT: 15 kg (33 lb)
HEIGHT: about 93 cm (36½ in)

These measurements are only averages. Boys tend to be taller and slightly thinner than girls.

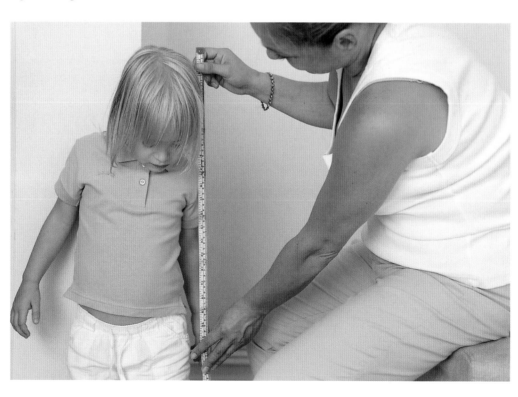

In early childhood, bones also knit together more quickly after an injury. A 3-year-old's broken thigh bone (femur) heals in 6 weeks instead of the 12 weeks it takes an adult. Fortunately, few toddlers break a femur, and most of your child's injuries should be minor. This is just as well, considering how adventurous the average toddler can be.

Knees and feet

At 2½ years, your toddler often stands with her feet wide apart. She may still have knock-knees until she is 3 years old. This is normal, although it is more obvious in some children than in others.

At 2½ years, your toddler's feet are still flat, but they are changing quickly. From about 3 years, her muscles and ligaments become stronger, which alters the flat shape of her feet so that arches gradually appear. By now, all the bones in her feet have proper bone rather than just cartilage. But these bones

don't all solidify until your child is about 18 years old. This is one reason why it is so important for her shoes to fit well right through childhood and adolescence. It is a good idea to check your child's shoe size every 2–3 months while she is 3 years old, as she will not notice, let alone tell you, if her shoes are getting too tight.

Her shoes should be the same shape as her feet, but they need to be protective rather than supportive. The bones and muscles of the foot will provide all the support your toddler's arches need. If your child has feet of average width, then you don't need a special width fitting, but you won't know this until you have her feet measured properly a few times.

Choose shoes that are easy to put on, though remember that slip-on styles also tend to slip off while playing. Give your child a say in the choice, especially if the shop has more than one pair that fit her well.

Immune system

During the first few years of life, your child's immune system matures fast as she encounters many different viruses and bacteria. You can give a child protection against serious viral infections, such as poliomyelitis and measles, and bacterial infections, such as tetanus and Haemophilus influenzae B (Hib) through immunization, but there are no routine vaccines against minor infections, such as the common cold. Your child can only gain immunity to these through the tedious process of coming across the virus.

There are many hundreds of different cold viruses, and the immune system has to learn to recognize and fight each one. This is why colds are so common in children. Each one can last 3 weeks, and it is not unusual for a toddler to have six or more colds a year, especially once she starts nursery or playgroup.

Care – feeding, sleeping and dry nights

Your toddler is making great strides in feeding and sleeping, although his increasingly active imagination may lead to nightmares. He is also beginning to be dry at night.

Feeding

At 2½ years, your toddler probably has a good appetite, but probably has likes and dislikes. If he rejects a particular food, don't give it to him for a while. When you serve it again, try a different recipe; he may not like the texture of macaroni cheese, but he may enjoy pasta bows with tomato sauce.

From 2½ years onwards, he can probably wield a knife and fork, and start eating from a plate as opposed to a baby bowl. Encourage good eating habits by eating with him whenever possible. Long meals strain a toddler's patience, but the occasional meal in a restaurant may actually bring out the best in his manners.

Sleeping

At about 2½ years, your toddler usually sleeps well, thanks to his active days. Some toddlers talk in their sleep, but this is nothing to worry about, although it may interfere with your peaceful nights.

Bedtime

Many toddlers like to stay up past their bedtime in case they miss anything. If timing is important, keep to your rules. Give your toddler 20 minutes' notice of his impending bedtime. It also helps to make your own late-evening activities sound dull. Decide whether or not to let him keep the light on.

At about 3 years, some toddlers may put off sleeping because they dislike the dark. Make your child's bedroom cosy and inviting, with his favourite things at hand, and possibly a dim night-light. A bedtime story is a good way of unwinding, and you can then can tuck him in and leave.

Nightmares

From about 3 years, nightmares are common. If your child wakes up in distress, cuddle and reassure him, give him a little time, then settle him back into his bed.

Nightmares don't mean that your child is disturbed or unbalanced, but they can reflect something that he has heard or seen. Don't let him watch scary television programmes or videos, or read him overly exciting stories before bedtime. If he is afraid of intruders, reassure him by explaining that home is a safe place, the doors are locked and only friends and family can get in.

Dry nights

By 3 years, many toddlers are dry at night, although some don't become dry until the age of 4 years or more. At least one in ten 5-year-olds still wets the bed on a regular basis. Boys often learn bladder control later than girls.

Starting off

Don't rush things. Wait until your child has good bladder control during the day, say a 3-hour interval between visits to the toilet, and also sometimes has a dry nappy when he wakes in the morning.

Without pressurizing him, find out if he wants to do without a nappy at night. The decision should be a joint one. Before you go ahead with this, cover the mattress with a protective plastic sheet and use bedding that is easy to wash.

Before bedtime

A trip to the toilet before bedtime is a must. Many parents also put their toddler on the potty again later just before they themselves go to bed. This is a good idea and helps prevent wet beds. However, you must wake your toddler for this. If he is not sufficiently alert enough to feel his bladder emptying, he will still be passing urine in his sleep, albeit not in the bed.

If your toddler's bladder is empty, staying dry overnight is no great achievement. Therefore, there is no point in restricting his drinks before bedtime, but avoid fruit juices, fizzy drinks and caffeine-based drinks. These can over-stimulate the bladder (and, in any case, a toddler should not be having tea or coffee).

Keep a potty near the bed, in case your toddler needs it in the night. A dim night-light and nightwear that's easy to remove will make things less difficult. You might also like to keep a pair of dry pyjamas and a change of bedlinen handy to save you hunting around in the night.

If your toddler still wets the bed

Be patient and deal with the problem as routinely as possible.

☐ Change the bed without fuss. Getting angry is counterproductive and unpleasant for your child.

☐ Expect some setbacks during holidays, or after the arrival of a new baby or following a house move. However, see your doctor if your child wets the bed after being dry for many nights. It could be a sign of a urine infection.

☐ Enuresis (incontinence) alarms can work well but they are usually designed for children aged 7 years or more.

Motor development

Your toddler's balance is good at 2½ years, and her muscles are better developed too. Her movements therefore gain in both power and precision. She still takes a tumble every so often, of course, but you may also notice that she can sometimes brace herself to stop a fall.

Walking, running and jumping

At 2½ years, your child walks well, swinging her arms more like an adult. For effect, she may sometimes make exaggerated arm movements. Now she rarely falls, even when she is busy looking at something else, as she often is.

By 3 years, your toddler is likely to run well, and to turn when she needs to.

She can also jump far better by now, and she uses both feet. However, when she wants, she can now stand on one foot for a few seconds.

Stairs and steps

At 2½ years, your toddler probably copes with stairs by using both feet on each tread. By 3 years, practice has paid off and she can go upstairs using one foot on each tread.

Encouraging movement

Many toddlers are very active and constantly on the move. You can encourage your child's activities while still considering safety and appropriateness.

- Help your toddler make the most of her muscles and movement in less hazardous settings. Baby gym and dance sessions, like tumble-tots, is a lot of fun for toddlers aged about 2½ years.

- Play music at home and encourage her to move in time to it.

- Let your toddler burn off excess energy on swings and slides, preferably in areas where there are cushioned surfaces. Indoors, a play tunnel can be fun.

- Take your toddler swimming. Most young children love splashing about in a pool.

- At this age, your child is much more amenable to logic and reason, so talk her through the possible consequences of, for instance, a fall off the playground roundabout. It is more effective and more educational than saying 'Because I say so'.

- Some elementary road drill is helpful. You cannot trust your child with traffic for years yet, but this early instruction is still valuable.

- Let your child walk to places with you when she feels like it, instead of riding in her buggy every time. Reins can be useful if she is not good at holding hands.

However, she is likely to put both feet on each tread on her way down, and may do so until the age of 4 years.

As well as being a lot quicker on the stairs, she also tends to jump off the bottom step. Some youngsters even like jumping off two or more stairs when going down.

Climbing and exploring

A lot depends on personality, but the average 3-year-old is very active, spending much time exploring and putting her improved motor skills to good use. Climbing could well be one of your toddler's favourite pursuits. Some like scaling trees, others favour climbing frames, garden fences, or any other object that looks as if it might be a fun challenge.

You can warn your toddler about safety and, if appropriate, about property damage and similar considerations, but there is no point in trying to stop her altogether. It is best to accept that a toddler will be naturally adventurous and so to then dress her accordingly.

Ball and other skills

At 2½ years, your toddler can kick a ball, although it may not go exactly where she had in mind. By 3 years, she may kick a ball more accurately. There is a lot of variation between children, but on the whole boys are better at kicking than girls, even at this early age.

At 2½ years, a toddler usually tosses a ball only a short distance. By the time she is 3 years old, she can throw a ball further and without losing her balance in the process.

By 3 years, your toddler can probably ride a tricycle properly, using the pedals instead of putting her feet on the ground. This is a fun way of getting around the park or playground. Even under your supervision, she is unlikely to be able to pedal safely all the way there and back, however, unless your home is very close to the park and the pavement is unusually level.

Hand–eye coordination

Toddlers are known for being impulsive. Even so, 2½–3 years is a time when your child puts a lot of thought and care into his actions. This makes him capable of far more delicate tasks than before, an important development that will please you both.

Making and building

As your child gets older, his skills are increasingly interlinked. Together with his improving concentration and persistence, your toddler's hand–eye coordination means that he can now build ever more complicated things. At 2½ years, he can construct a tower of eight or more bricks. By 3 years, his tower could be much higher before it topples over.

At 3 years, he can also make more interesting things. If you show him how to make a bridge out of three bricks, he will quickly grasp the idea. Before long, he is building whole streets and towns out of his bricks and spending long, happy stretches of time engaged in a world of his own make-believe.

Drawing and painting

At 2½ years, your toddler may still hold a paintbrush or crayon with his fist. By about 3 years, if not before, he is far more likely to hold either of these like an adult. This makes him capable of much more. He now draws or paints spontaneously. At about 3 years, he

does not just have fun making random marks: the marks he makes can be edges or boundaries. He learns to make enclosed areas and can begin to create basic shapes, which is an important advance in his creative activities.

About the age of 3 years, your toddler can imitate you drawing a circle. He can also copy a circle that you drew earlier. If you ask, he may draw a person, a house or a car for you. You may not always recognize the fruits of his labours, and he may still not spend very long on each drawing or painting, but even so his skills have come on a long way.

Dressing, undressing and using the toilet

At 2½ years, a toddler can often dress and undress himself on occasion. Don't worry if your child cannot do this yet. The important thing is that he shows an interest. Once he does this, all you need to do is give him the opportunity and he will learn in his own time.

By 3 years, your toddler can generally manage to take off and put on his clothes, except those with very fiddly zips and buttons. When these defeat him, his frustration can be almost palpable, but he is willing to learn. Now is also a good time to instill some tidiness and teach him that clothes should not be left in a heap on the floor. He will be happy to put them either away in the drawer or in the dirty linen basket if you make a game of it, say by taking turns to deal with one item of clothing each.

When it comes to shoes and socks, taking them off is easy, so your toddler has been doing that for some time. By his third birthday, he can probably put on his shoes independently without problems as long as they fasten with Velcro rather than with laces or buckles. Allow him time to do things himself whenever you can. Your patience

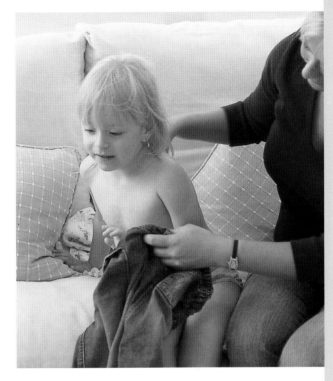

will pay off in the greater independence that he will display when he goes to playgroup or school.

By 3 years, going to the toilet is mostly a one-person effort too, unless you are needed for wiping. You may have to supervise hand-washing too, so that it gets done properly.

Around the house

Towards 3 years, your toddler becomes far more aware of the impact that he can have. He uses all his powers of observation to make his movements appropriate to the task. Now, he may even be able to carry something fragile, such as a china bowl. Setting the table for dinner may bore you, but not him. He wants to be helpful and takes pride in being 'grown-up'. Time your request right, and choose a task within his capabilities, and he may turn out to be an eager assistant around the house, fetching, carrying and doing little jobs that make him feel important.

Senses and learning

As she heads for her third birthday, your toddler's improving concentration and memory allow her to learn many new things. Now, thanks to her reasoning skills, she is also receptive to simple logic.

Concentration and memory

A toddler's concentration really comes on apace from 2½ years, so she stays on-task when something interests her, whether it is building with her bricks or playing a game with you. However, she may still leap from one thing to another when she is very excited.

Between 2½ and 3 years, she has a good memory, especially for things that appeal to her. She recalls events of last month and even longer ago. If you tell her that she can have, say, an ice cream tomorrow, she is most unlikely to forget this the next morning.

By 3 years, largely thanks to her powers of retention, she knows many colours by name.

She may also recognize some letters, although it is too soon to expect her to know the whole alphabet.

Groups and numbers

Your toddler at 2½ years is already aware of groups of things, such as buildings, animals and vehicles. She can also pair related objects, such as a cup and saucer, or a chair and table.

Learning to count is a complex business with many facets. There is evidence that even young babies have some appreciation of number. Simple experiments with cards show that they can easily distinguish between two dots and three dots. Other studies suggest that infants can do elementary sums. There may be special brain circuits responsible for dealing with numbers, and their level of development may have some genetic basis. It is no surprise that children learn about numbers and counting at different speeds, and that some show from early on that they have a 'head for figures'.

Youngsters vary as to when they learn to count out loud, but from 2½ years your toddler may be able to recite numbers in the right order. She can almost certainly remember a sequence of digits such as 'one, two, three', and repeat them after you. By 3 years, she may be able to count up to five.

Logic and reasoning

From 2½ years, your toddler's powers of logic are noticeably better, and from 3 years onwards you can begin to reason with her, at least some of the time. When you tell her to do (or not to do) something, tell her why. She not only deserves an explanation, but is also more likely to cooperate in future if she understands that there is a logic behind what you say.

Play and learning

Adults tend to think of play as leisure, but it actually serves a serious purpose (see page 13). Now that your toddler's concentration, memory and logical thinking are developing fast, she can manage sustained play that forms a basis for her further learning.

Even a pursuit that is not overtly educational has value because it teaches a child to stay focused – a vital skill for life. Youngsters who do not play much can have trouble learning later. This is one reason why it is important to let your toddler play. Naturally, you cannot disrupt your own plans because she has just taken her favourite toys out of the cupboard, but whenever possible let her get on with playing without rushing or distracting her.

Stimulating your toddler's learning

There is no point in cramming learning into your child. It is more a matter of giving her opportunities to fulfil her potential.

- Talk to her about her activities before and afterwards. Planning and reviewing helps a child to learn.

- Playing picture lotto can refine her powers of observation and teach her about matching and non-matching things.

- Help her to learn about related objects by, say, looking at items in old home-shopping catalogues and cutting them out.

- Simple dominos help your toddler learn about numbers. You can get colourful domino sets that appeal to young children.

- If you want to introduce the alphabet to your toddler, make it fun with a jigsaw or lotto. Show her lower-case letters rather than block capitals, because that is what she will learn at nursery and school.

Imagination and creativity

Both boys and girls are highly imaginative. The world of make-believe in all its forms takes up a lot of your toddler's time from 2½ years onwards. As he comes up to 3 years, your child will spend more and more time playing on his own, and soon he will make friends of his own age.

Routine

A little structure in the day helps stave off boredom. As well as letting him have his own time to immerse himself in play, try to have an outing every day to let your child experience new things and to let off steam. Periods of quiet play with you, perhaps with a puzzle or crayon and paper, help to vary the tempo.

Role play and dressing-up

Any kind of role play is valuable for your toddler because it helps him to experiment with different situations. Helping himself to old clothes in a dressing-up box or suitcase can keep him entertained for ages. The costumes need not be expensive or elaborate, and what you already have can easily be supplemented with a few jumble-sale items.

You may want to consider some special props, such as a toy stethoscope or a pirate's eye-patch. Sometimes your toddler will want you to play his make-believe games with him, while at other times you should take a back seat. You will soon be able to sense what he needs from you. Try to avoid taking over his play, however much fun it may look.

Tidiness and order

Playthings should live in a toy-box or cupboard when they are not being used. Having all his toys out at once actually distracts a child from his play. Mess creates stress for you, and it also poses physical dangers because you or your child could trip and fall.

At 2½ years, a toddler is not too young to learn about putting things away. In fact it can instil in him a sense of ownership and responsibility. It does not happen overnight, so you will have to encourage and help him. Putting things away in the right place together is a good opportunity for him to learn about sets and groups of things.

Encouraging creativity

Provide your toddler with paper, crayons and paints. He will also enjoy modelling clay or dough, and maybe dry pasta shapes to paint or glue onto card to create artistic masterpieces. Cooking can be creative too, and your toddler may enjoy cutting shapes to bake biscuits or icing cakes with you. Don't spend a long time setting up modelling or painting, or you may be disappointed. Despite the strides in your child's development, at 2¹/₂ or even 3 years he still cannot concentrate for anywhere near as long as you can.

A toddler can make plenty of mess in a short time, however.

- A little paint or clay can go a long way, so protect his clothes before he starts.

- Put your most easily damaged possessions out of the way.

- Protect the floor with plastic sheeting or old newspapers.

- Let your child play out-of-doors whenever possible.

- Schedule really messy activities for just before bathtime, or when you were going to wash the kitchen floor anyway.

- He needs to learn boundaries, so teach him where he is allowed to paint or draw and where it is forbidden. A blank wall is almost irresistible and most toddlers make at least one attempt to draw on the walls. Some parents are happy to designate one wall for their child's self-expression.

Computer games

Some games are aimed at the very young, but this does not necessarily make them a good idea for a toddler. At this age, a child does not need to learn keyboard skills. Using computer games may help develop a child's visual discrimination, coordination and reaction times, but there are other more sociable ways of doing this. Sitting at a screen tends to be poor for posture and, depending on how long a child spends, may affect his eyesight too. Games are imaginative, but they make use of someone else's imagination, not your child's. Before you invest in computer games, bear in mind that they don't help a youngster socialize or deal with the real world, and they can also be habit-forming.

Communication

At 2½ years, your toddler has an extensive vocabulary and is determined to use it. Talking with increasing fluency and expression, from now on she is in a phase when she prefers to use speech rather than actions to get her thoughts across.

Understanding and meaning

Your child's comprehension is more advanced than her speech. By 3 years, she understands almost everything you say. She can, however, also make herself understood to most people, although her pronunciation is still immature. Typically, a 2½-year-old misses out consonants such as 'k', 'n' or 't' at the end of words. At 3 years, your toddler may still lisp.

Her grammar is not yet perfect either. She may sometimes make strange plurals such as 'childs', or incorrect past tenses such as 'eated', but given time she will learn.

Remembering and reciting

At 2½ years, your toddler remembers and recites nursery rhymes. She can repeat a string of three or so numbers, and by 3 years she may be learning to count (see pages 210–11).

She probably repeats words and phrases that she hears you say, especially if they are unfamiliar. This is normal until the age of 3 or 3½ years, and helps a child to learn new words and assimilate their meaning.

Linking words and sentences

Your toddler knows and uses important link words. By 2½ years, she uses the word 'and', enabling her to make longer and more complex sentences. She also knows 'today' and 'tomorrow'.

By about 3 years, if not before, your toddler speaks in five-word sentences. She understands and uses the word 'yesterday'. She may even know the days of the week. Language and thought are inextricably

Stimulating your toddler's language skills

There is no substitute for talking to your toddler. Try to answer her questions patiently. If you tell her you will answer later, keep your promise.

■ Use an adult tone of voice, although you may still have to exaggerate the pronunciation of words from time to time.

■ Talk too about feelings, which will enhance your toddler's grasp of more abstract words.

■ Watch what you say in front of her. Young children have a habit of picking up bad language at the wrong moment.

■ Use books to enrich her experiences. Watching you read on your own helps as well. Families in which adults read for pleasure tend to raise children who enjoy books too.

linked, and your child's mastery of words helps her to plan as well as review her activities – an important part of learning.

Wanting to know more

By 3 years, your toddler will be chatty and wanting to know about everything. Her favourite word may well be 'why'. You will know the answer to most of her questions (except perhaps bizarre ones, such as 'Why is blue?'). For those that you cannot answer off the top of your head, it does no harm to say you are not sure and will find out. The fact that you can use books or the Internet to find out things is a useful message to get across to your child.

Soon, she may be asking you where babies come from. There is no need to go into a lot of detail at this age. Your child probably needs a simple answer along the lines of 'From Mummy's tummy'. Bear in mind that the word 'where' can have subtly different meanings. If she asks where she came from, she may just want to know which town she was born in.

Emotions

At 2½ years, your toddler still shows great spontaneity, but he is becoming more thoughtful and considerate. Towards 3 years, he is more aware of other people's emotions and moods. He is not just more independent, he is increasingly mature all round.

Relationships with other people

Your toddler has gained a good sense of himself in relation to others. He may enjoy talking about family members and how they relate to each other. By 2½ years, he has no trouble realizing that the person in the mirror is himself. Towards 3 years, he may enjoy looking at his reflection.

Now your 2½-year-old is less self-centred. He is interested in what other people think, especially those close to him. He may read your facial expressions to gauge what is appropriate behaviour. You may also hear him speculate about how strangers feel.

Sometimes, he will strike up conversations with strangers. There is little trace now of his former shyness. For his own safety, it is a good idea to teach him never to talk to people he does not know unless you are with him.

By 3 years, your toddler has some sense of other people's point of view, and he responds to their distress. Girls tend to do this more readily than boys.

Relationships with other children

Your toddler is very interested in other children, including babies. By 2½ or 3 years, he instinctively uses a higher pitched voice and simpler sentences to a young baby. Around now, he will behave appropriately with children of different ages and he may spend a lot of time playing with them. At about 3 years, he is ready to make genuine friends outside the family.

Kindness and sharing

Kindness is not entirely natural, in the sense that it has no obvious evolutionary advantage. Even so, by 3 years your toddler may show great consideration for others. He will, for instance, be happy to share things without being asked and may offer one of his toys.

Your 3-year-old is also mature enough to take turns, which makes games possible. There are, of course, times when he will not be in the mood, so it is best not to expect too much.

At about 3 years, your toddler is often kind and gentle with animals. If you have a pet, he may already appreciate that it is more

easily hurt than he is. If he is interested, give him some responsibility for the animal, such as changing the dog's water bowl or feeding the goldfish. Supervise him, especially with a dog, as children can be clumsy. A cat is likely to scamper off if someone treads on its tail, but a dog might turn around and bite.

Tantrums

Your toddler is finding other ways to deal with negative feelings, so from about 2½ years he usually has fewer tantrums. This does not mean his responses are always reasoned, however. When he cannot handle his feelings, he still has the odd outburst, but it is now unlikely to last as long.

After a tantrum, he may appreciate that his outburst actually gained him nothing. Because he is now more amenable to logic, you can begin to talk together about emotions and the things that may make him angry or upset.

Dealing with fears and phobias

From about 2½ years, some children develop fears, such as fear of dogs or the dark. It is easy, but seldom helpful, to tell a toddler not to be silly. It is best not to make fun of your child's fears. Instead, be gentle and reassure him. Give him the option of, say, a dim night-light to counteract his anxiety about the dark, or put a light switch within easy reach of his bed. If dogs intimidate him, be there to calm him the next time he sees the neighbour's poodle.

Play down your own fears (of spiders, for example) as much as possible because it may influence your toddler. Fears and phobias are not hereditary, but your own experiences can affect your child. If your toddler's fear persists or it interferes with daily life, talk to your health visitor about other strategies that might help.

Starting nursery or playgroup

Towards her third birthday, your toddler is much more outward-looking and ready for the stimulation of brand-new experiences. Pre-school offers a new environment in which to play, learn and make friends. Although you are still the most important influence in her life, once she starts attending nursery or playgroup, the time spent with children of her own age increases in significance.

Choosing the right time

Your toddler is ready for nursery or playgroup when she is happy to be away from you for short periods and is able to communicate with other children and adults. This is usually between 2½ and 3 years, although some youngsters are more self-reliant than others.

It helps if your toddler is independent at toileting. Many nurseries will not accept a child who is still in nappies. For this reason, as well as their greater emotional maturity, girls are often ready before boys.

The arrival of a new baby in your family may not be a good time because your toddler may prefer to stay close to you. Children differ, though, and you are the best judge of when your toddler is ready. If she is still clingy and dependent on you, leave it for a while.

Choosing the right nursery or playgroup

Nurseries tend to be more structured and may be attached to a primary school, whereas playgroups are more informal.

However, there is a wide variation, and it pays to look closely at all the pre-school provision in your area well in advance.

You can tell a great deal from the atmosphere, the space available, the toys and equipment, and whether the children seem to be contented. Ideally they will look happily occupied and not bored or running riot completely.

Follow your instincts, but ask questions too. Apart from basics, such as hours and costs, you should also ask about the following aspects.

• What level of supervision is there? And what is the child-to-adult ratio?
• How structured are the activities? Do the children have a choice?
• Is there a progression of activities, for instance are there different groups for the older children?
• Are girls and boys treated the same?
• Are parents expected to help out on a rota basis?
• How do the staff deal with misbehaviour?

Preparing your toddler

Tell your toddler about going to pre-school, but don't overwhelm her with detail. Take her to see the nursery or playgroup, especially if she has not been there before. Well before she starts, make sure that she can manage her shoes and the toilet with minimal help. If she has a favourite soft toy, reassure her that Flossy Bunny or Little Ted can go with her if she likes.

The first few days

As well as taking any comfort object, pack a bag containing a complete change of clothes for your child and hand it to the staff as you arrive. Mishaps with toileting are common, especially when a child first starts pre-school.

Your toddler may be able to attend part-time for the first couple of weeks, just to get used to it. You will probably want to stay with her for the first session or two, but keep your distance and fade into the background if possible. If you leave the premises, be sure to say goodbye and tell her that you will be back later. There may be a few tears to begin with, but this usually passes quickly. It is far more upsetting for a toddler to look up and find that you are not there when she was expecting to see you.

Always make sure that the staff can reach you in case of emergency, and be on time to collect your child. Let her tell you about her morning. It is probably not a good policy to tell her what an exciting time you had, as she may wish she had been with you.

The next step

That first day at nursery or playgroup may only be a couple of hours long, but it is a significant experience in your child's life. New horizons are now opening up for her as she stands on the threshold of the big wide world.

Index

Acknowledgements

Executive Editor: Jane McIntosh

Editor: Kate Tuckett

Executive Art Editors: Rozelle Bentheim, Darren Southern

Design: Beverly Price, one2six creative

Senior Production Controller: Manjit Sihra

Photographer: Adrian Pope

With thanks to the Early Learning Centre for the loan of toys.
Look online at www.elc.co.uk, place an order by phone 08705 352 352
or visit one of the stores.

With thanks to Daisy & Tom for the loan of nursery equipment.
Browse online at www.daisyandtom.com or visit one of the stores.

Special Photography: Octopus Publishing Group Limited/Adrian Pope

Other Photography:
Alamy/Dennis MacDonald 32; /thislife pictures 11
Bubbles/Stephen Wade 20
Corbis UK Ltd/Owen Franken 33; /ER Productions 21
Getty Images 132
Angela Hampton/Family Life Picture Library 22, 23
Homebase 104
Octopus Publishing Group Limited 179 bottom left; /Peter Pugh-Cook
126, 195; /Adrian Pope 105 bottom left, 210; /Russell Sadur 5 bottom
right, 15, 17, 18, 19, 34, 37 bottom left, 40, 42, 43, 57, 64, 67, 68, 69, 72,
73 bottom left, 80, 81, 84, 87 bottom left, 89, 93, 94, 103, 105 top right,
107, 111 left, 111 right, 115, 117, 118 top right, 119, 130 bottom left, 131,
137, 178, 180, 193, 197, 203, 204, 206, 209, 213, 214, 216, 219
Photodisc 135
Science Photo Library/Dr. Najeeb Layyous 10; /Ron Sutherland 31